Shut Down the Business School

"drum beat"

Shut Down the Business School

What's Wrong with Management Education

Martin Parker

PLUTO PRESS

First published 2018 by Pluto Press
345 Archway Road, London N6 5AA
www.plutobooks.com

British Library Cataloguing in Publication Data
A catalogue record for this book is available from the British Library

ISBN   978 0 7453 9917 1   Hardback
ISBN   978 0 7453 9916 4   Paperback
ISBN   978 1 7868 0239 2   PDF eBook
ISBN   978 1 7868 0241 5   Kindle eBook
ISBN   978 1 7868 0240 8   EPUB eBook

This book is printed on paper suitable for recycling and made from fully
managed and sustained forest sources. Logging, pulping and manufacturing
processes are expected to conform to the environmental standards of the
country of origin.

Typeset by Stanford DTP Services, Northampton, England

Simultaneously printed in the United Kingdom and United States of America

Contents

Acknowledgements

Thanks to all the audiences who have made generous comments on these ideas at various talks in various places over the past decade. Particular thanks to David Castle from Pluto for commissioning the book. Partly because of the long gestation of this work, as well as my laziness and lack of creativity, various chunks, fragments and flakes have been stolen from some earlier pieces. The main ones are: 'Managerialism and its discontents' in S. Clegg and C. Cooper (eds) (2009) *The Sage Handbook of Organizational Behaviour: Volume II. Macro Approaches*, London: Sage, pp. 85–98; 'The architect and the bee revisited: Managing, organizing and agency' in A. Fuad-Luke, A.-L. Hirscher, C. Kuebel and K. Moebus (eds) (2015) *Agents of Alternatives: Re-designing Our Realities*. Berlin: Agents of Alternatives e.V., pp. 362–371; '"This is water": Labours of division, institutions and history' in C. Steyaert, T. Beyes and M. Parker (eds) (2016) *The Companion to Reinventing Management Education*, London: Routledge, pp. 497–509; 'Organizing is politics made durable: Principles and alternatives' (with G. Cheney, V. Fournier and C. Land) in A. Spicer and G. Baars (eds) (2017) *The Corporation: A Critical Interdisciplinary Handbook*. Cambridge: Cambridge University Press, pp. 538–545, and 'Alternatives to management ideas' in A. Sturdy, S. Heusinkveld, T. Reay and D. Strang, (eds) (2018) *The Oxford Handbook of Management Ideas*. Oxford: Oxford University Press. A very quick rehearsal of one of the ideas can be found as 'Schools for organizing' in D. Barry and H. Hansen (eds) (2008) *Handbook of New Approaches to Management and Organization* London: Sage, pp. 213–214, which was expanded into 'Towards an alternative business school: A school of organizing' in B. Czarniawska (ed.) (2016) *A Research Agenda for Management and Organization Studies*. London: Edward Elgar. An early version of the argument is prefigured in Chapter 9 of my book *Against Management* (2002) Cambridge: Polity.

And this book is dedicated to my dad.

Preface

Business schools have huge influence across the Global North, yet they are also widely regarded to be intellectually fraudulent places, as well as being implicated in producing the culture of short-termism and greed which has led to innumerable business scandals. This short book proposes that they should be closed down, and replaced with a something that I will call the 'school for organizing'. Most business schools exist as parts of universities, and universities are generally understood as institutions with responsibilities to the societies they serve. Why then do we assume that degrees in business should only teach one form of organization – capitalism – as if that were the only way in which human life could be arranged?

My proposal in this book requires substantial intervention in the governance of universities, and questions the increasingly common assumption that they are simply institutions which should respond to what students and employers want them to provide. I also assume that what gets taught and researched at universities matters, in the sense that it influences what students think, and hence shapes the horizon of the societies that we live in. If we want to be able to respond to the challenges that face human life on this planet, then we need to research and teach about as many different forms of organizing as we are able to collectively imagine. For us to assume that global capitalism can continue as it is, means a path to destruction. So if we are going to move away from business as usual, then we also need to radically re-imagine the business school as usual. And this means more than pious murmurings about corporate social responsibility, the crocodile shedding tears while its jaws tighten on your leg.

Saunter around the average university campus nowadays, and it's likely that the newest and most ostentatious building will be occupied by the business school. Because that's the point. The business school has the best building because it makes the biggest profits (or, euphemistically, 'contribution' or 'surplus') – as you might expect, from a form of knowledge that teaches people how to make profits. Of course, there are plenty of critics of the business school – conservative voices bemoaning the *arriviste* MBA, employers complaining that its graduates lack practical skills, Europeans moaning about Americanization, and radicals wailing about the concentration of power in the hands of the running dogs of capital. To add to the clamour, from 2008 onwards, there were plenty of commentators suggesting that business schools were complicit in producing the crash, teaching selfishness and the engineering of fiendishly complex financial instruments that no one really understood. There are a few people offering solutions to the problem of the b-school, but most shy away from radical restructuring, and instead tend to suggest a return to (supposedly) more traditional business practices, or a form of moral rearmament decorated with terms like 'responsibility', 'diversity' and 'ethics'. All of these suggestions leave the basic problem untouched, that the business school only teaches one form of organizing – market managerialism.

That's why I think that we should call the bulldozers in and demand an entirely new way of thinking about management, business and markets. If we want those in power to become more responsible, then we must stop teaching students that heroic transformational leaders are the answer to every problem, or that the purpose of learning about taxation laws is to evade taxation, or that environmental costs are external to supply chain logistics, or that creating new desires is the purpose of marketing, and so on. In every case, the business school acts as an apologist, selling ideology as if it were science as part of one of the longest public relations campaigns in history.

What might a different sort of research and teaching agenda look like? To put it rather bluntly, how can the discipline of 'management' stop being mere advocacy and become a proper field of enquiry? My answer is to propose a 'school for organizing', as an academic discipline and political practice that is intended to discover a different world, not merely reproduce the one that we have. Organizing is all around us, and it is a topic of enquiry which clearly overlaps with other parts of the social sciences and humanities – sociology, anthropology, politics, history and so on. The school for organizing wouldn't need its own shiny building to stress its distinctiveness, because it would have to work with teachers and researchers who could show us variety and strangeness, rather than endless recitations of the same. No form of organization would be off-limits, so we might imagine courses and research projects on the circus, families, queues, city-states, utopias, villages, sects, matriarchies, mobs, gangs, cities, clubs, segmentary lineage systems, pirates, the mafia, Occupy and the Apollo moon landings. Why would the study of literature not be relevant to the understanding of organization? What lack of imagination allows us to think that we can learn nothing from the initiation ceremonies of secret societies, the baking of cakes for a village fair, or the nine orders of angels in a celestial hierarchy?

Organization is the ground and consequence of human behaviour, the patterning that allows us to become what we are, and what we will be. Yet this generous conception of 'organizing' is made invisible because the business school building already marks out and naturalizes a very particular field of enquiry – one that assumes the corporation as the only important organizational form. Even a cursory glance at history shows that human beings have organized themselves in a vast variety of patterns. These patterns vary across space and time, being shaped culturally, politically, spiritually and so on. In fact, the multiplicity of differences seems to far exceed any similarities, unless we remain at the highest level of generalisation. Faced with such a dizzying range of specific procedures and devices, we might try and learn from this multiplicity. If we want to understand how to produce forms of organizing that provide us all with nice things to eat and do, interesting people to talk to, and varied places to go, then we have a rich range of successes and failures to look at. It would be sensible to learn from what other people have already tried, unless we really think that we are the cleverest people who have ever lived and that the intellectual spaces marked out through the arrangements of the contemporary university are actually reflected in the world outside.

Many business schools and their professional associations and cheerleaders have been busily trying to avoid this or any other unpleasant conclusion, as inequality widens and the climate changes. Their only suggestions for reform appear to involve modules on ethical leadership and corporate social responsibility. ('Business' ethics being somehow different from the sort of ethics that the rest of us practice, and corporations implicitly in need of any sort of responsibility.) Of course, a reluctance to change is perfectly comprehensible. Careers are being made, the toilets need repainting, and the vice chancellor keeps demanding a bigger contribution to the bottom line. But if the business school is to rescue its tarnished image and begin to address the challenges that face us all, then it needs more than a bit of re-branding. It needs to become a proper academic discipline, and change its name from being a statement of tribal affiliation.

Because we do need some place in the university where questions of organization are studied and taught. Whether youth club or multinational company, issues of co-ordination and control are central to our lives. This isn't only a matter of thinking about the 'soft' aspects of business either, because understanding organizing also includes thinking about money, about making things and moving things, and about the law (and hence also about the state). However, the legal, technological and financial issues which shape organizing must be taught in a way that does not separate them from political and ethical choices. Economics, accounting and finance are not neutral techniques which can or should be taught as if they were context free. So, ideas about 'markets', 'efficiency', 'productivity', 'profits' and so on must always be understood as contingent social agreements, not naturally occurring phenomena which are subject to timeless laws. Including the environment, equality and ethics into such forms of calculation does not pervert them, rather it clarifies their purpose.

To this must be added the broader political issues that are necessarily part of any patterning of power, and the danger of those who come to believe that they are the cleverest people who have ever lived. In *The Republic*, written around 380 BCE and one of the first examples of a fully realized utopia, Plato suggests that great attention needs to be paid to the education of leaders, in case they become tyrants, because the temptations of power are multiple. We have seen that often enough in the last two-and-a-half millennia, and the single-minded pursuit of wealth and power rarely seems to produce positive outcomes. So perhaps it's time to take the arrogant atriums down, and for schools of organizing to encourage modesty and historical understanding in their graduates and researchers. If this means they study how orchestras are organized, and the leadership required in running a feminist dried bean co-operative, then so much the better. Some of the aspirations of a liberal view of the university might even be saved, as noisy debate and discussion replace the complicities and silences of the plush lecture theatre. At least the students will understand that there are alternatives, that the business school of the Global North isn't the final word concerning knowledge of organizing. The school for organizing can then find its place as a legitimate part of the university, not just a cash cow and Ivy League finishing school.

THIS BOOK

This is a short book, so I will be proceeding without much care, preferring polemic to detailed analysis. It is, however, based on over two decades working in UK business schools, and on quite a lot of reading and writing, so for those readers who want to know more, the endnotes should provide what you need.[1]

I will begin by drawing a lurid picture of what goes on within the business school, because I can't assume that all my readers will have visited one. (Indeed, I rather hope that most of you haven't; otherwise I really am just preaching to the choir.) After that, I will clarify just what gets taught within the business school, stressing the ways in which it offers a kind of hidden curriculum which demonstrates a kind of triumphalism about management and markets. After that follow two chapters which lay out what a variety of critics have said about management and about the business school itself. This is followed by a chapter which suggests that the business school is a parasite that is transforming the university itself, producing a new way of understanding just what the university is and does. That brings us to the end of the first part of the book, in which I have piled up the complaints and hopefully persuaded you that we should start collecting firewood to burn the whole thing down.

The second part of the book offers the alternatives, and brings you back from the darkness. It begins with a chapter in which I ask just what management is, and what managers do. This leads into perhaps the hinge for the book, my insistence that the term 'organization' is a much more useful one if we want to talk about how human beings come together to do things. So rather than relying on all the baggage that comes along with ideas about business and management, let's begin again with the school for organizing. Chapter 8 discusses the politics of the school for organizing. There are innumerable ways in which people have organized, but they are not all equally desirable, so how might those teaching and researching organizing and organizations think about what to include and what to exclude? The penultimate chapter tries to persuade you that students will want to study at the school for organizing, before I conclude with some thoughts about the future of education in organizing. But before we get to those sunny uplands, I need to show you what the problem is, so come with me into the atrium.

I

What goes on in business schools?

Imagine walking up to a new building somewhere near you, just some sort of anywhere in some city in the Global North. There is a Starbucks nearby, and you can hear the sound of a motorway. There has been rain. The parking was tricky. The grass has been cut, the trees are well behaved and the shrubs are obediently trimmed. The architecture is generic modern – glass, panel, brick. It could be the office for any knowledge company on any office park near any somewhere. Outside, there's some expensive signage offering an inoffensive logo, probably in blue, probably with a square on it. The door opens, automatically. Welcome to my world.

Inside, there's a female receptionist dressed office smart (not too much makeup and a smile on the lower half of her face) and some crouching sofas with business magazines on even lower tables. Some abstract art hangs on the walls, and perhaps a banner or two with some hopeful assertions: 'We mean business.' 'Helping you to get ahead.' 'Teaching and Research for Impact.' Shiny marketing leaflets in classic modern fonts sit snugly in dispensing racks, with images of a diverse tableau of open-faced students on the cover. MBA, MSc Management, MSc Accounting, MSc Management and Accounting, MSc Marketing, MSc International Business, MSc Operations Management – an alphabet of mastery. Less prominent will be some leaflets for undergraduate degrees and PhDs, or perhaps a DBA, MPA, MRes, DSocSci. This is a qualifications dispensary, with an acronym for every need and easy payment options.

Inside, a lot of hard surfaces cause the conversations to bounce around. Easy to clean, but hard to hear a whisper. A coffee shop – perhaps that was the Starbucks, or perhaps it's another Starbucks – which also sells smoothies, wraps and has fruit by the till. A sign suggests that you should pick a healthy option! Take the stairs! Go for a walk at lunchtime! A big screen will be somewhere over the lobby, running a Bloomberg news ticker and advertising visiting speakers and talks about preparing your CV. A glass lift leading to floors with endless runs of corridor leading to hundreds of doors – Professor this, Dr that – interspersed with noticeboards with the front covers of books and first pages of articles. Elsewhere there will be plush lecture theatres with thick carpet, perhaps named after companies or personal donors. The lectern bears the logo of the business school. In fact, pretty much everything bears the weight of the logo, like someone who worries their possessions might get stolen and so marks them with their name. Unlike some of the shabby buildings in other parts of the university, the business school tries hard to project efficiency and confidence. The business school knows what it is doing and has its well-scrubbed face aimed firmly at the busy future. It cares about what people think of it.

So do the students of course. The people bustling around this place are mostly well dressed, and you don't see many tattoos, earrings, or T-shirts screaming adolescent outrage. A lot of the students are Chinese, Indian, Asian, African and they aren't dressed like the rest of the social science students in the university. Haircuts are tidy, jewellery is understated, Doc Martens and high heels are not in evidence. Mostly, people are hanging around in groups, trying hard to look as if they are having a good time, or being serious about their studies. Those that aren't are intent on laptops or smart phones, trying not to look like they have no friends. There is no music, just the sound of earnest conversation and footsteps bouncing off hard surfaces.

That's what it is like in my imaginary b-school. Even if it isn't really like that – if the roof leaks a little and the toilet is blocked – that is what the business school dean would like to think that their school was like, or what they would want their school to be. A clean machine for turning income from students into alumni and profits, or 'contributions' if the school is part of a university, which most are. My office is on one of those corridors – housing a well-paid professor who teaches students from far away and writes articles that few people ever read.

As I said in the Introduction, I hope that most of the readers of this book won't have been inside a business school, so I am going to begin with a bit of background. Before I convince you what is wrong with them, I need you to understand what business schools are, and why they matter. This will involve some history and some context, but most importantly I want you to know what these places feel like. I want you to feel the echoes in the atrium, and begin to hear what students and staff talk about in the lecture theatres, coffee shops and offices. I want to convey the combination of smugness and insecurity that hangs around these places, with their corporate art, glossy brochures and inspiring slogans. I will also say something about how much money they make, and why this matters.

But first, since most business schools are part of universities, we need to understand just how they have changed too.

DOORS TO KNOWLEDGE

One of the most impressive buildings at Oxford University is the Old Schools Quadrangle of the Bodleian Library, which dates from 1613. It's a gorgeous golden stone structure, and looks like it has always been there, solidly emplaced in the cobbles and harbouring generations of scholars. For the camera-clicking tourists and the self-consciously trotting students who rush impatiently across the square, there is no question that it belongs, that it deserves to always be here. Setting aside its unshakable confidence as a building, there is something else that catches the eye as you stand in the courtyard, a series of beautiful blue doors with a golden serif-lettered sign above them in Latin: *Schola Moralis Philosophiae, Schola Logicae, Schola Naturalis Philosophiae* and so on. They look like props from the Harry Potter films, so much mystery do they promise. Their reason for being there was that each discipline once had a single room, and the doors are still marked with the subject. On the ground floor: Moral Philosophy, Grammar & History, Metaphysics, Logic, Music, Natural Philosophy. On the first floor: Law, Greek, Arithmetic & Geometry, Astronomy, Rhetoric, and Anatomy & Medicine. Doorways to knowledge, institutionalized in stone.

How could it be otherwise? We need to know what we are going to get in the lecture theatre so that we know which lecture theatre to go to. Universities, like libraries, must advertise their classifications. How could we have a library in which all the volumes were jumbled up in piles, like a crazy second-hand book shop with no logic, no filing system, no way of finding what you want to read? Knowledge could be lost in such places, put aside one day and not found for decades. Classification matters to the university. You can't just go to one and study, because you have to study something that has already been identified as a field of study. That is to say that the structure of the institution prefigures what is knowable, and allocates space and resources accordingly. Not that these categories are timeless. Those which made sense four hundred years ago are different to those we recognize now. So some subjects have expanded and divided, such as Natural Philosophy and Astronomy, whilst others have shrunk and congealed, like Moral Philosophy, Metaphysics and Logic. Still other areas are entirely new: Anthropology, Geography, Psychology, Sociology and so on.

Other things haven't changed. In order to collect the books and build the library, Sir Thomas Bodley – son of a merchant, career diplomat, and husband to a wealthy wife – had to collect a lot of money. Like most of the ancient universities of Western Europe, the generosity of kings, bishops and merchants was required in order that stone and wood could be carved and pheasants cooked for table. And, just like nowadays, generosity often likes to be noticed, so Bodley ensured that it would be:

> He had prepared a handsome Register of Donations, in vellum, in which the name of every benefactor should be written down in a large and fair hand so all might read. And he kept the Register prominently displayed so that no visitor to the library could escape seeing the generosity of Bodley's friends. The plan, as it deserved, was a success, for its originator found that, 'every man bethinks himself how by some good book or other he may be written in the scroll of the benefactors.'[1]

And the money and books poured in, from the Earl of Essex, Lord Buckhurst, Lord Hunsdon, Lord Lumley and many others. Universities have always been dependent on benefactors, on flattering the powerful of any given age. Though they have occasionally been places where dissent has been sheltered, or even revolution fomented, for most of their history universities have been places that responded enthusiastically to those with money and power, naming colleges, buildings, lecture theatres and chairs after those who open their purses. They have tended to be conservative places, sites for the reproduction of knowledge, not its generation.

THE *SCHOLA COMMERCIA*

Bodley's library shows us that the door to knowledge is a particular door, not a general one, and it requires money and power to build it. Further, the university isn't a door in itself, but it contains many different doors. They don't go to anywhere and everywhere, but to particular places. Indeed, the geography of any university is a guide to its classification systems, to what it collects together and what it keeps apart, with science areas and arts areas; social science towers, floors, or corridors for specialisms and special research units in special buildings. The spatial and temporal distribution of knowledge is written across the campus, with ivy-clad stone for the old and glass-clad concrete and brise-soleil for the new. Probably the most significant addition to most universities in the Global North in the last fifty years has been the *Schola Commercia*, the Business School.

So what is taught in the business school lecture theatre? One example will suffice for now, that of Warwick Business School in England, a place which appears to have embraced the idea that theirs is a form of knowledge which changes the world, and that should therefore be sold for premium prices. In a text with echoes of medieval theology in its 'visions' and 'missions' we find a description of what we can find if we open this door:

Our Vision & Mission

Our vision is straightforward. What underlies everything is academic excellence, and the impact it has on society.

Our vision.

- To be the leading university-based business school in Europe.

Our mission.

- To produce and disseminate world-class, cutting-edge research that is capable of shaping the way organisations operate and businesses are led and managed.
- To produce world-class, socially responsible, creative leaders and managers who think on a global scale, regardless of the size of their organisation.

- To provide a lifelong return on investment for our students and alumni.[2]

Some features of this knowledge are worth drawing attention to. First, we might observe that 'academic excellence' is asserted to be the practice which underpins everything that takes place within this business school, though this has been qualified (with an insertion which was added several years after the original 2010 version of this statement) with the idea of making an 'impact on society'. Quite apart from the political good sense of nodding to the UK government's introduction of 'impact' as a measure of excellence in the current state audit of research, this insertion might also be taken to qualify the previous clause, and to suggest that the academic excellence which matters is that which has impact, and not that which is speculative or ivory tower. Further qualification is provided by the 'vision', which tells us that the institution is in competition with other 'university-based business schools' in Europe, and specifies that it is going to be the best one in the region. On what criteria is unclear, but we can probably assume that this will be measured by league tables and the like, because some sort of metric must be used if the term 'leading' is to have anything other than rhetorical force. The 'mission' section further qualifies the claim about competitive and impactful research, because it tells us who the customers are – 'leaders' and 'managers'. These are people who think on a global scale, and who consequently require research that is up to date and amongst the best in the world in order to support their leadership and managing of organizations. The final sentence suggests a particular orientation to this knowledge, since it is articulated as an investment which will provide a return. That is to say, the customer will purchase the knowledge with their money and time, and it will repay them. It seems safe to assume that this return will be economic, given the tone of the rest of the text.

In a text like this, we find a particular understanding of the relationship between knowledge and students, an assumption about who those students are, an implication about the market that business schools trade in, and a series of qualifications which allow us to understand that research is excellent when it helps leaders and managers (and the order is significant) have an impact on the world. Perhaps we could read this statement as a series of claims about what the school does *not* do (which might be the only way to give it some distinctive meaning). Business schools do not teach knowledges or practices as an intrinsic good; do not teach workers, citizens, or activists; do not collaborate with other schools, and do not pursue research which helps workers, citizens, activists to have an impact on the world. If you want those forms of knowledge, go elsewhere.

The point of this rather extended textual torture is to underline the idea that there is a relationship between forms of knowing and the organizational structure of institutions. That is, the idea of the university as a timeless institution where certain liberal values are taught is evidently misleading because the contemporary university does not have one orientation to knowledge, but many. Probably the only generalization we can make is to say that it is a machine for generating divisions and distinctions, made concrete in the long walk from the physics department to the philosophy department, or the ramifications of the committee structure. As the anthropologist Mary Douglas has suggested, institutions can be treated like brains, structures that encourage certain forms of thinking whilst quietly making other connections difficult, unthinkable, even heretical.[3] The mere fact that the business school is on the edge of campus, and has its own cafe, is itself a way for an institution to think. So is the fact that the last time I was there, Warwick Business School, on the ground floor of one of its clinically white atria, had a large etched plastic plaque on the wall which gratefully listed its corporate benefactors and wealthy donors.

A BIT OF HISTORY

In terms of the long history of the university, the business school is a recent invention, though even the University of Oxford has one now. Pretty much every university has one now. In 1996, Oxford's Saïd Business School was generously endowed by a financier and businessman who brokered the £43 billion Al Yamamah arms sales by the United Kingdom to Saudi Arabia in the 1980s.[4] So even if universities have been around for a millennium (Bologna was founded in 1088), the vast majority of business schools only came into existence in the last century. Despite loud and continual claims to have been a US invention, the first is probably the École Supérieure de Commerce de Paris, founded in 1819 as a privately funded attempt to produce a 'Grand École' for business, and which was bought by the Paris Chamber of Commerce in 1869.[5] The ESCP was established by the businessman Vital Roux, with help from the economist Jean-Baptiste Say, both advocates of the importance of unfettered free trade.

Roux himself was particularly interested in how citizens were to be trained in the arts of business, and in 1800 he published a book entitled *On the influence of government on the prosperity of commerce.*[6] In his book, he explicitly suggested that French schools of commerce needed to be established and that, as their primary teaching method, they should engage in business simulations. One year later, J.-P. Boucher (a professor of law in Bordeaux) published a book on the organization of commercial institutions in which he also encouraged the state-sponsored development of business schools. The first chapter was titled 'On Business Schools and their methods of organization; the Educated and the Ignorant Merchants'. Despite the political complexities of post-Revolutionary and Napoleonic France, the growth of the mercantile classes, combined with a modernizing humour, meant that the idea of a scientific form of education in commerce was here to stay. It was widely perceived that the ignorant merchants needed educating. In 1806, Boucher put forward a project for the establishment of a business school in Paris, and Roux wrote a report approving the proposal. However, despite wide circulation, neither the government nor the chambers of commerce were interested, and it took Roux another decade to persuade two wealthy silk merchants, Brodart and Legret, to eventually fund the École Spéciale de Commerce et d'Industrie, which opened with about sixty students. By 1828, the school had 104 students on its courses, and they were an international bunch, including students from England, Belgium, Switzerland, Prussia, Austria, Russia, Portugal, Spain, Italy, Greece, Africa and eight from America.[7] The school taught economic liberalism, a form of thought which many imagined as necessarily attached to political liberalism, as well as subversive internationalism. As a result, police surveillance caused continual problems. An institution which now comfortably represents vested interests began as something of a challenge to post-Napoleonic nationalism.

All these early business schools were European – not American. The state-funded Institut Supérieur de Commerce d'Anvers and the Jesuit-funded Institut Saint-Ignace École Spéciale de Commerce et d'Industrie were both founded in 1855 in Antwerp. Two years later, Budapest Business School was founded, followed the next year by the Ca' Foscari University on the Grand Canal in Venice. Two more French schools followed in 1871, the Rouen Business School and ESC Le Havre. It's a little odd then that the dominant story is that North America invented the b-school, an account which probably has more to do with the language of those writing the histories of the institution over a century later.

The first US business school is usually considered to be the Wharton School of the University of Pennsylvania in the US, established in 1883. Joseph Wharton (1826–1909) was

an American industrialist who invested in mines, railroads, a
fish factory that produced oil and fertilizer, a modern forestry
planting operation, and cranberry and sugar beet farms and zinc
and nickel manufacturers. He was also a major shareholder in
the Bethlehem Steel Company (later the employer of Frederick
Taylor, the man who invented 'scientific management'). In other
words, Wharton was a very wealthy man, which was odd given
his Hicksite Quaker background. The usually rural followers of
Elias Hicks tended to be hostile to the modern economy, seeing
it as a corrupting influence. When, in 1881, Wharton donated
$100,000 to found a School of Finance and Economy, he insisted
that the school advocate protectionism, as well as

> ...to provide for young men special means of training and
> of correct instruction in the knowledge and in the arts of
> modern Finance and Economy, both public and private, in
> order that, being well informed and free from delusions upon
> these important subjects, they may either serve the community
> skillfully as well as faithfully in offices of trust, or, remaining
> in private life, may prudently manage their own affairs and
> aid in maintaining sound financial morality: in short, to
> establish means for imparting a liberal education in all matters
> concerning Finance and Economy.[8]

There is a moral tone to this prospectus, a hope that scientific
education will prevent business from being corrupt, and produce
upright citizens to serve a nation that needed to pull together
after a brutal civil war.

Despite these nineteenth-century beginnings, the growth of
business schools is essentially a twentieth-century phenomenon:
the Warsaw School of Economics was founded in 1906, Harvard
Business School in 1908, Stockholm in 1909. In North America,
hugely wealthy business donors gave money in return for naming
rights and by 1936, there were nearly two hundred business

schools in the US alone.[9] Virtually every major city in North America and Western Europe had a business school by the 1970s, and from the 1950s onwards, we also see an equally rapid growth in other parts of the world: the University of Pretoria in 1949, Renmin in China in 1950, Delhi in 1954, ESAN University in Lima in 1963 and so on. Whilst the growth in European business schools tended to be characterized by expanding departments within publicly funded universities, other parts of the world commonly developed private stand-alone institutions, with North America having a mixture of both.

In 2011, the American Association of Collegiate Schools of Business estimated that there were then nearly 13,000 business schools in the world.[10] India alone is estimated to have 3,000 private schools of business.[11] Pause for a moment, and consider that figure. Think about the huge numbers of people employed by those institutions, about the armies of graduates marching out with business degrees, about the gigantic sums of money circulating in the name of business education. In 2013, the top twenty US MBA programmes already charged at least $100,000, with executive variants being half as much again.[12] At the time of writing, London Business School is advertising a tuition fee of £75,000 for its MBA. Of course, most schools can't charge that much, so if we take my last employer as an example (because I happen to know these figures), a mid-size business school in a provincial university in the UK, then do the maths, rounding down and converting to US dollars, business schools globally must have an income of *at least* $400 billion. Add to this the market for accreditation agencies, textbooks and journals, the information corporations who sell data, and data about data, a global conference circuit and the people who make the mortarboards and gowns. Add to this again a huge black market in predatory journals and customized essay-writing websites and you have an awful amount of money at stake, both above and below the line. No wonder that the bandwagon keeps rolling.

CRITICISM AND THE BUSINESS SCHOOL

A man is visiting some cannibals and is astonished to see this sign outside a restaurant:

> Today's specials:
> *Brain of engineer: $15*
> *Brain of architect: $20*
> *Brain of MBA: $250*

> He says to one of the waiters: 'Wow, an MBA's brain must be so delicious!'

> The waiter replies: 'Are you kidding? Do you know how many MBAs you need to kill to get just a little bit of brain?'

I am by no means the first person to have criticized the *Schola Commercia*. Indeed, in popular culture, the business school is now shorthand for some combination of greed and stupidity. In the *Futurama* episode 'Mars University' from 1993, Farnsworth, a splendidly mad scientist, is having a conversation with Gunther, a monkey who has been wearing a hat that makes him very clever. At the end of the episode, he decides that the hat caused more trouble than it was worth:

> *Farnsworth*: But what about your super-intelligence?

> *Gunther*: When I had that, there was too much pressure to use it. All I want out of life is to be a monkey of moderate intelligence who wears a suit. That's why I've decided to transfer to business school.

> *Farnsworth*: Nooooooooooooo!

In pithier one liners, the MBA is said to stand for 'Mediocre But Arrogant', 'Management by Accident', 'More Bad Advice', 'Master Bullshit Artist' and so on. Add to this general sarcasm some more pointed accusations about business schools being production lines for greed and immorality, responsible for the 2008 crash and so on, and you have a fairly toxic diagnosis.

But these are external criticisms, and what is remarkable about the b-school is just how much criticism has also come from inside the schools themselves. For example, in the last decade, and particularly in North America, we have been presented with a different sort of history. This is not a triumphalist history of growth, but a story of loss, of the ways in which the civic virtues of the early schools (such as Wharton), or the modernizing technocratic ambitions of some of the later ones, were washed away by tides of money from the 1970s onwards. This can be told as an account of how the business school began to isolate itself from the social sciences and humanities more widely and instead began to bow the knee to neo-classical economics and behavioural psychology. Or it documents how a series of moral and political aspirations became subordinated to the idea that managers are just agents for shareholder value. Or a concern with how management predicated on evidence-based policy becomes subverted by neoliberal economics and the financialization of everything. Mie Augier and James March, both US business school academics, even finish their book by suggesting that the post-Second World War period was a 'golden age' for the business school. Presumably referencing the myth of the brief Kennedy presidency, they conclude 'But, briefly, there was Camelot.'[13] Other books subtitled with phrases such as 'unfulfilled promise' and 'lost foundations' create the impression that the early US business school was a place for the cultivation of professionals, the encouragement of virtues and an education in practical matters.

This may well be the case, but these rather nostalgic histories point up a very pervasive sense of a tragic fall from grace in the contemporary business school. They tell us more about now than then. The diagnoses vary, but this is generally a story of corruption. Of business school presidents and deans following the money, of teachers giving the punters what they want, of researchers pumping out paint-by-numbers papers for journals that no one reads, and students expecting a qualification in return for their cash (or more likely their parents' cash). And most business school graduates won't become high-level managers anyway, just precarious cubicle drones in anonymous office blocks, or wall-eyed cyborgs in call centres.[14] And these are not complaints from professors of literature or sociology, state policy makers, or even outraged anti-capitalist activists. These are views in books written by insiders, by employees of business schools who themselves feel some sense of disquiet or even disgust at what they are getting up to. I don't want to overplay this, because (as I will show in the next chapter) most work within business schools is blithely unconcerned with any expression of doubt, participants being too busy oiling the wheels to worry about where the engine is going, but the internal criticism is significant nonetheless.

The contrast between the shiny leaflets in the shiny buildings and the expressions of doubt is clearest in the field usually called 'Critical Management Studies' (CMS). ·A term coined in the early 1990s, it now brings together a large number of academics – mostly in Europe but in other parts of the world as well – who have been biting the hand that feeds them for quite a few decades, sometimes gnawing it so obsessively that it is surprising that they find any meat left on it at all. And CMS has done very well for itself. Certain schools, superstar professors, journals, conferences, textbooks and so on have made what once seemed 'outsider' into something rather insider. In terms of publications, there is a reader, a companion, a handbook, a key concepts book, a four-volume set of readings, several journals with 'critical' in their title, and even (with a breathtaking lack of modesty for an area only two decades old) a 'classics' collection. To these core readings, we can add books on 'critical' research methods, critical approaches to strategy, marketing, quality management, accounting and just about every other category of knowledge offered by the business school.[15]

The problem is that these insiders' dissent has become so thoroughly institutionalized within the well-carpeted corridors that it now passes unremarked, just an everyday counterpoint to business as usual. Careers are made by moaning softly, rocking gently, or wailing loudly in books and papers about the problems with the education offered by business schools. The b-school is described by two CMS insiders as 'a cancerous machine spewing out sick and irrelevant detritus, justified as "practical" and glossed up as "business relevant". [...] It extorts fees from the middle and upper classes so that it can stamp their offspring with a passport into corporate sleaze, mortgage slavery, burn-out, stress, overwork and repression'. Even titles like *Against Management*, 'Fucking Management' and 'The Greedy Bastard's Guide to Business' appear not to cause any particular difficulties for their authors. I know this, because I wrote the first two.[16] Frankly, the idea that I was permitted to get away with this speaks volumes about the extent to which this sort of criticism means anything very much at all, or is really just a fart in a thunderstorm. In fact, it gets rewarded, because the fact *that* I publish is more important than *what* I publish.

Which is why I wrote this book. I wanted to try to produce something which clearly stated what I think is wrong with business schools and the education that they provide, but then not merely trundle off into the usual nostalgic platitudes about what universities *should* be doing. As if the stone of the Old Schools Quadrangle would provide timeless cover for a liberal education, or reading lots of critical social theory would make people behave better. (An argument which is usually a cover for professional self-interest, and which ends up saying nothing about what should be done about and within the b-school.) Neither did I want to write another article that no one will read, either because it is hidden behind a publisher's paywall, or because it is written as an intervention into some academic debates and is hence strangled with references and trying to sound clever. There is a bigger question here too, because the university has increasingly become the business school, and if we want to change the b-school, then we need to consider the question of the university as well. The doorways to knowledge matter, and we might decide that the ones we have are not fit for purpose, and should have different signs above them.

But more of that later. In the next chapter, I want to be more precise about just what I think is wrong with business schools, because it's not enough to moan about moderately intelligent monkeys in suits, entertaining though such a characterization is. What is actually taught in the business school?

2

Teaching capitalism

'Then,' I said, 'because the work of our guardians is the most important of all, it will demand the most exclusive attention and the greatest skill and practice.'

'I certainly think so,' he said.

'And will it not need also a nature fitted for this profession?'

'Surely.'

'Then it will be our business to do our best to select the proper persons and to determine the proper character required for the guardians of the city?'

'Yes, we shall have to do that.'

'Well, certainly it is no trivial task we have undertaken, but we must be brave and do all in our power.'

Plato, *The Republic*

HIDING IN THE LIGHT

What do business schools teach? What are the contents of the courses? What skills or knowledge do they convey? In one way, this is a simple question. We could look at the descriptions of the courses and see what the titles of the modules are. This is in itself an exercise in Mary Douglas's institutional thinking, because it gives us a structure of classification – a way of dividing different parts of the world of management. More on this later, but this isn't the only thing that the business school teaches.

Much writing on education has explored the ways in which a 'hidden curriculum' supplies lessons to students without doing so explicitly.[1] From the 1970s onwards, various critical researchers on primary and secondary education explored how social class, gender, ethnicity, sexuality and so on were being implicitly taught in the classroom. In the most obvious sense, this might involve segregating students into separate classes – the girls doing domestic science and the boys doing metalwork, for example, or the working-class kids doing motor maintenance or gardening and the middle-class kids doing physics or literature. These are lessons being conveyed about the differences between women and men, and what might be expected of children from different backgrounds. The hidden curriculum can be taught in other ways too, in the architecture or age of the buildings, by the ways in which teaching, learning and assessment are practiced, or through what is or isn't included in the curriculum – Shakespeare but not comics, imperialism but not slavery and so on. The hidden curriculum tells us what matters and who matters, which places are most important and what topics can be ignored.

A huge amount of work has been done on trying to deal with these issues in the educational materials provided to teachers in many countries in the Global North. Materials on black history, women in science, or pop songs as poetry are now fairly routine. That doesn't mean that the hidden curriculum is no longer a problem, but the contents of many lessons are now at least more inclusive and make an attempt to represent different standpoints on the subject matter at hand. In many of the more enlightened educational systems, it is not now routinely assumed that there is one history, one set of actors, one way of telling the story. But in the business school, both the explicit and hidden curricula sing the same song. The things taught and the way that they are taught generally mean that the virtues of capitalist market managerialism are told and sold as if there were no other ways of seeing the world.

The intellectual and practical problem for the business school is at heart the problem of governance. As Plato says in the epigraph to this chapter, we need to be careful how we educate those who might lead us. He is writing about those who will be in charge of his ideal city, and recognizes the importance of ensuring that such people are moderate, compassionate and wise, that their characters are suitable for cultivating the sort of society that we wish to live in. After all, if we educate our graduates in the inevitability of tooth-and-claw capitalism, it is hardly surprising that we end up with justifications for massive salary payments to people who take huge risks with other people's money. If we teach that there is nothing else below the bottom line, then ideas about sustainability, diversity, stakeholders, responsibility and so on become mere decoration. The message that management research and teaching often provides is that capitalism is inevitable, and that the financial and legal techniques for running capitalism are a form of science. This combination of ideology and technocracy is what has made the business school into such an effective, and dangerous, institution.

WHAT DO BUSINESS SCHOOLS KNOW?

The business school was made by acts of organizational classification. Of course we could also tell a story about students' and policy makers' demand for the knowledges that might be used to run capitalism and a technocratic state, or (in some states, such as the UK) the need for income for universities facing a gradual withdrawal of state support combined with strong encouragement to find income streams from elsewhere. Or we could emphasize the role of industrialists themselves in endowing universities and building their legacies in ivy-clad stone. As I suggested in the previous chapter, there are some excellent accounts of the growth and development of the business school, particularly in the US, but any understanding of what sort of knowledge is thereby produced must also tell a story about how a particular field of enquiry was demarcated through deploying new divisions of the old and unities of the new. 'Management', as a subject, didn't spring into existence, fully formed: it had to be assembled from many bits and pieces.

In order to produce a subject, it needs to be distinguished from other subjects. It needs to make space for itself, and claim distinction from forms of expertise that already exist. A gap needs to be found, and widened, in which the new discipline can grow, recognizing itself and being recognized by others as doing something new, not merely repeating the same. From the late nineteenth century onwards, we have the beginnings of a productive differentiation in much of the Global North which generates 'Management', 'Business', 'Commerce' as topics, though this assemblage is made with different components in different places at different times. What the new discipline used depended on what was already there, and hence what resources could be used and what spaces needed to be opened. In the UK, the whole process occurs relatively late, with a curriculum fashioned from bits and pieces from pre-existing fields such as sociology, industrial relations, psychology, accounting and economics (all themselves categories of knowing which we don't find in the Old Schools quadrangle).

The establishment of a new disciplinary area could never be something which happens rapidly because it involves aligning many elements. Teaching and research staff must first come from elsewhere and then establish the academic infrastructure which supports a discipline, and which makes academic labour recognizable. This includes modules, courses, degrees, PhD students, workshops, conferences and so on. A professional association must be established – this will organize bigger conferences, give prizes, perhaps publish a journal or two. Validating bodies might be established to provide badges of quality for marketing purposes, or lobbying associations propose that common interests across the sector are best navigated collectively in return for an annual fee. This latter might also offer training courses, whether cascading best practice with expert speakers or discussing collective dilemmas, also in return for a fee, and at a nice hotel somewhere sunny, or at least interesting. Commercial publishers might begin to see opportunities in expanding numbers of students and so establish a separate list for the new subject. They then begin to solicit and sell textbooks, handbooks, companions, dictionaries, academic monographs, and more journals. Universities must make space within their existing buildings, or construct new ones. The wealthy might be encouraged to ferret around in their deep pockets and have their names or the names of their companies attached to buildings, lecture theatres and professorships. After a while, the apparatus is experienced as timeless, as being a necessary part of the way in which the practice of the discipline is conducted. As the PhD students graduate to teaching and research positions so is the business school then staffed by people who have not come from elsewhere, and do not have personal experience of a different configuration of knowledge.[2] Students are in turn taught by people who have done business school PhDs, and people inside and outside the institution begin to recognize the b-school as a particular sort of place which deals in particular kinds of knowledge.

But the labour of division doesn't end here, because as it grows, the knowledge in the b-school is further divided into departments – Strategy, Marketing, Finance, Accounting, Operations and so on – each of which become recognizable as distinct intellectual concerns, often with their own conferences, journals, textbooks and so on. Within the new building, each domain acquires its own corridor – perhaps a group, division, or department. The granularity of knowing doesn't end there either, of course, because fine internal distinctions then become deployed to understand the particular orientation that individuals or groups might have towards their subject matter, such as those that – in the area that I teach and research – operate to distinguish organizational behaviour, organizational theory, organization studies, human resource management, organizational psychology, industrial relations, employee relations and so on. Fully socialized inhabitants of the institution will often find it hard to explain to outsiders just what these distinctions mean, and why they matter at all.

DIVISIONS OF KNOWING

Let us consider the main distinctions which produce the curriculum of the business school, because there isn't really a subject taught called 'Management' or 'Business', any more than there are university courses on 'History' or 'Biology'. By which I mean that any academic subject is really an aggregate of its various component sub-disciplines, and it is only taught as if it were a single thing in schools, not universities. So what are the components of business?

Knowing about people

One way to begin might be to make a distinction between the different elements that are required to imagine a business operation – human beings, money, a product or service, some technology and so on. Let us begin with the human beings. They are described in a subject often called 'organizational behaviour', and the name carries an important modifier. This is a subject which is intended to consider how people behave within organizations, by which is meant formal work organizations in which those people are employees or managers, and not in other contexts. Its implicit bet is that there is something distinctive about this sort of behaviour, as opposed to the sort that might happen outside the formal organization – in the family, on the street, with friends, at leisure. Furthermore, the sorts of organizations that are usually considered are almost always capitalist businesses, and not voluntary organizations, sports clubs, charities, worker cooperatives, choirs, or political parties.

So the contents of organizational behaviour are produced by excluding things, which is quite understandable in terms of the need to establish boundaries around a subject area. What is less often remarked upon is the way that the exclusions also produce a certain model of the person as the employee of a capitalist firm. That is to say, someone who is attached to other human beings by wages, by a legal contract, through authority relations which determine the times and spaces of behaviour as well as the conduct of that behaviour and so on. This is clearly a very specific way of being a human being, and it excludes much about those human beings which is not deemed relevant for those contexts. Indeed, it proposes an idea of human beings as creatures that exist in distinctive spheres of activity, belief and behaviour, with the separation of those spheres being more important than their interconnection.

That separation, signalled by the prefix 'organizational', has some effects that are worth spelling out in a bit more detail. On one side, it means that a great deal that might be important in thinking about human beings is effaced, made invisible, or irrelevant. The family, the home, the school, leisure, social class, sexuality, the state are all domains of activity which are not routinely considered to be germane to explaining what people are like at work. Now there is a sort of experiential truth to this, because it is clear enough that there are separations between our work role and our other roles, and these are often enough experienced as tensions, limitations, or repressions. Yet that isn't at all the same as saying that there actually *is* a separation. In fact, the very existence of stresses suggests that the connections are all too real, whether they involve the problems of fitting childcare around work, the rapid promotion of people who have been to the right universities, or a decision as to who to tell that you are gay.

Now because these issues, and many, many others, are not routinely considered to be part of the teaching of organizational behaviour, the version of human beings which is taught ends up being rather an odd one. It might be summarized as something like 'rational egoism', which is not exactly the same as the 'economic man' often modelled by economists, but it comes close. Organizational behaviour does not assume that people are only motivated by money, though that is quite correctly understood to be one of the ways in which they are motivated. In addition to money, though, a variety of other terms are proposed as needs with various relations and intensities, as attractors to which people are pulled. These might include 'status', 'power', 'meaning' and so on, all concepts which then become understood as goals of individual human decision making. This certainly complicates the idea of a person as a robot in search of cash, and has produced a variety of interesting theories about the relationship between different variables, often resulting in diagrams of triangles, diamonds, or boxes with arrows connecting them.

The rational egoist makes choices about what they want most, that is to say, they calculate their preferences and make decisions about action accordingly. This might involve balancing desires, like accepting a lower-paying job because it provides more status, or being more likely to ask for a raise if the job has less meaning. The point is that they are rational, in terms of their calculations of interest at any particular moment, and they are egoistic, in the sense that their decisions are aimed at maximizing their own interest. Most famously perhaps, Abraham Maslow's 'hierarchy of needs', suggests that lower-order needs must be fulfilled before higher-order needs can be addressed, in the sense that if we are hungry, it's difficult to concentrate on the spreadsheet.

Now in a specific sense, organizational behaviour isn't wrong. Its observations and questionnaires have been used to generate some descriptions that might be helpful, all things being equal. But outside the world of quadratic equations, all things are never equal. Maslow's work, for example, was one element in a much larger humanistic project, not aimed at explaining anything specifically organizational at all. Indeed, many of the terms and examples which he uses to explain the 'higher' needs – 'love', 'belonging', 'esteem', 'self-actualisation' – could not possibly be imagined to be only satisfied within a work organization. It seems to me that Maslow's work was actually reduced into a form that would make sense for rational egoists when it entered organizational behaviour, and then became a staple part of the curriculum for generations of students. Another way of saying this is to suggest that the persons imagined to be the objects of business school knowledge are not much like the persons that most of us know. It is difficult to imagine them making a model boat out of matchsticks, laughing at the misfortunes of others, dancing in the street, or stroking the hair of a child. A poet would barely recognize these persons as human beings at all.

Knowing about other things

Having begun with the idea of rational egoistic behaviour in organizations, noting as we go just what a narrow subject that is, we can continue on to describe the other parts of the b-school curriculum. There are national and local variations here, but I think it's fair to say that these are the central elements of most general business and management qualifications. I'll go through each in turn, simplifying as I go and offending my colleagues as I proceed.

Accounting is largely an attempt to systematically describe the movements of cash and credit within and between organizations. It is predicated on the assumption that the purpose of accounting information is to produce better control systems for management through 'management accounting' – the clue is in the name – and useful information for managers, investors and regulators in the field of financial accounting. It is worth noting that the interests of these three groups may not be the same, a fact which often leads to the production of different versions of the truth for different purposes. Some forms of accounting are intended to minimize tax liabilities, a skilful and well-compensated job, whilst others are aimed at disguising problems that might deter investors. There is little or no interest in 'worker accounting' within business schools, because it seems to be assumed that they would not need, or perhaps understand, such information. Neither is there much interest in social issues, civil society, or the environment. Accounting only provides accounts for certain sorts of people, and for certain sorts of purposes.

Finance is a field concerned with understanding how people with money invest it. It assumes that there are people with money, or capital that can be used as security for money, and hence it also assumes substantial inequalities of income and wealth. The greater the inequalities within any given society, the greater the interest in finance, as well as the market in luxury yachts. Finance academics almost always assume that earning rent on capital (however it was acquired) is a legitimate and perhaps even praiseworthy activity, with skilful investors being lionized for their technical skills and success. The purpose of this form of knowledge is to maximize the rent from wealth, often by developing mechanisms (whether mathematical or legal) which can multiply it, or cause it to appear to be multiplied. Successful financial strategies are those that produce the maximum return in the shortest period, and hence that further exacerbate the social inequalities that made them possible in the first place.

Management Information Systems, like Management Accounting, is about producing knowledge for managers. In that sense, it assumes management as a cadre of people who know things about the organization that other people don't know, or are not allowed to know. The prefix embeds hierarchy, information asymmetry, and the likely surveillance of others – within or without the organization. It is premised on the sensible assumption that high-quality, relevant and timely information is necessary to make high-quality, relevant and timely decisions, but is agnostic about the direction or context of the decisions actually made. The objects of management information systems are those matters which can be quantified, or at the least codified in some way, such as accounting and finance information, geographical or temporal sales data, together with the results of survey data on employees, competitors, and potential or actual customers. It allows the managers in the organization to see the things that they want to see, and to imagine that their decisions are based on all possible data. As with accounting, there is no science of worker information, except in the sense of managers deciding what they want workers to know, and not to know.

Marketing is a discipline which considers how organizations sell the things and services that they produce. It assumes that consumers are rational egoists with certain preferences, and then develops theories to best connect to those preferences in order to get them to spend money. Marketing is predicated on the idea of maximizing the number or value of transactions within a given organization, market, or economy, and hence any mechanism which holds the distant promise of encouraging spending is worth investigating. Marketing could involve researching what people say that they want in order to design products or services that they will buy. It also involves communicating messages about the value of products or services in order to persuade people that they need them, or, if they already need them, to spend the maximum amount of money purchasing them. This means that marketeers have investigated the persuasive capacities of many forms of address – perceptual cues such as colour and volume, different channels of mass communication and person-alization, attachment to celebrities or social causes and so on. Like organizational behaviour, marketing attempts to develop a theory of motivation – in this case consumer motivation. Its success would be measured in behaviour change which results in spending patterns which benefit the people who have paid for the marketing in the first place, so successful marketing will also tend to concentrate income and wealth.

Human Resource Management is the application of theories of rational egoism to the management of human beings in organizations. It is what used to be called 'Personnel', but now contains this implicit claim that the 'human resource' is an input to organizing that might be paralleled by the 'technological resource', or the 'financial resource'. This is a telling displacement, largely because it places the human as an element to be used by management in order to produce a successful organization. Rather than being the end of organizing, or its fundamental precondition, the human is something to be engineered by using the sort of knowledge generated in organizational behaviour. Despite its use of the word, Human Resource Management is not particularly interested in what it is like to be a human being. This is a form of knowledge which is framed at an aggregate level in terms of propositions about the best tests to be used to recruit particular sorts of new humans; or how reward systems might be best designed to optimize human motivation; or the tensions between what managers would like to do and what any particular legal system prevents them from doing. Its object of interest are categories – women, ethnic minorities, the underperforming employee, the retiring employee – and their relationship to the functioning of the organization. It is also the part of the business school most likely to be dealing with the problem of organized resistance to management strategies, usually in the form of trade unions. And in case it needs saying, Human Resource Management is not on the side of the trade union, or the worker. That would be partisan. It is a function which, in its most ambitious manifestation, seeks to become 'strategic', to assist senior management in the formulation of their plans to open a factory here, or close a branch office there.

Innovation is an area which attempts to understand how to encourage the generation of particular sorts of novelty in certain forms of organization. In the simplest terms, it would ask how organizational structures, routines, or uses of technology encourage or discourage the production of new ideas. Novelty is here defined as something which can benefit the organization – perhaps a new product or service, or a new way of working to deliver products or services at cheaper cost or greater profit. Innovations, that is to say, changes, in the structure of ownership, the distribution of surplus, the quality of working life or wider social benefits, would not usually be understood to be part of this discipline. Innovation only counts as innovation, as recognizable novelty, if it produces something that customers will ultimately pay for, or, if it is to be applied in the public sector, that will result in more for less. So innovation isn't concerned with radical novelty in economic or social terms, but with less predictable moves within a predictable game.

Operations, or *Logistics*, is a discipline which models and controls the movement of materials and people within and between organizations. It often uses some complex mathematics, programming and technology in order to ensure that things can be moved from one place to another, arriving when they are needed. Much of the knowledge in this area was initially developed by the military, which first developed containerization, for example. Nowadays, the movements of products into supermarkets, parts for manufactured goods, raw materials and so on are elements in global production and consumption systems. Because this makes transportation cheap and fast, 'trade', as in the movement of things, becomes imagined as almost frictionless. The replacement of high-employment ports by low-employment container parks, distribution sheds, the development of roads big enough to take trucks, carbon emissions from shipping are the consequences of logistics. Amazon, and the relentless destruction of the small high-street retailer, is the result of logistics. This is a knowledge that is aimed at shrinking time and space, and when successful, destroys the local. It is also manifest in ideas like 'quality' and 'lean', when they are applied to processes within human systems. The intention here is essentially, like time and motion studies, an attempt to minimize the time that a person spends being unproductive and to ensure that there are no actions that do not directly add value to the organization.

International Business is usually a triumphalist area of the curriculum. It begins with a gleeful insistence that the local no longer matters, that economic globalization is inevitable, that the successful business leader must be an internationalist. Images of people striding through airports would be common on the covers of International Business textbooks. While such cosmopolitan views should clearly be celebrated, this is cosmopolitanism with a distinct purpose. The view of the international provided here is of nations as territories for conquest, of other regions or states being allies or obstacles to the expansion of a company or sector of the economy. This means that the discipline is one that considers cultural questions to be interesting only insofar as they can help or hinder global trading relationships. Cultural difference tends to be treated as something that needs to be mastered or smoothed out, with business relationships being the aim of such commensuration. The internationalization of business is simply assumed to be good, and perhaps inevitable. Carbon emission reduction targets, cultural or economic protectionism, local self-sufficiency and the role of trans-national corporations in shaping their legal and financial environments are matters which are largely ignored. The aim of international business is to produce a frictionless planet for the play of global capital.

Strategy is a slightly mysterious discipline, and this has given it a certain amount of prestige within the b-school. Its mystery comes from the idea that it is an attempt to predict the future, and then to shape an organization in such a way that it profits most from what that future looks like. As should be clear here, this is an activity practised by people with power, by senior managers who (by virtue of their elevation within the hierarchy) can supposedly see further than most employees. Two points are worth repeating here. One is that strategy assumes hierarchy. It assumes the inequalities of power which enable some to lead by pointing their fingers in particular directions while others merely follow. Strategy is never collective, never the outcome of deliberative or democratic processes, though its practitioners do often claim to have 'consulted' with 'stakeholders' at some point during their decision making. Second, the strategies that are discussed within this area are those that are aimed at benefiting certain 'stakeholders' and not all of them. That is to say, a credible prediction of and response to the future will be one in which owners, managers and shareholders maintain or advance their advantageous positions. A strategy which resulted in accruing advantages to other groups would be understood to be inadequate, not a strategy at all, but a concession of defeat.

It's also worth mentioning that the addition of the word 'strategy' to any of the other business disciplines has invigorating effects. Mere marketing looks dull in comparison to 'strategic marketing', and when HRM becomes strategic it moves to the next level. The addition of this word appears to have two related effects. One is that the discipline becomes putatively concerned with planning for the future and not dealing with the present, and hence that it becomes an area that leads, and does not merely sit behind a desk. This has the consequence of raising the pay and status of those who describe themselves in this way. Rather like the progressive distinction between administration, management and leadership – each of which makes the previous one sound like mere bean counting – strategy has managed to define itself as the sort of thing done in the executive suite, or at 'away-days' in a decent hotel. Sprinkling some of it on any other area hence produces miracles, by making whatever it has been applied to sound very much more important.

I'll finish this tour with *Business Ethics* and *Corporate Social Responsibility* – both attempts to deal with business as a problem, and pretty much the only areas within the business school which have developed a sustained critique of the consequences of management education and practice. These are domains that pride themselves on being gadflies to the business school, insisting that its dominant forms of education, teaching and research require reform. The complaints that propel writing and teaching in these areas are predictable but important – sustainability, inequalities of income and power, the externalization of various social problems, and the production of graduates who are taught that greed is good. Business Ethics is the area which diagnoses the problems, usually by using various forms of philosophically derived ethical reasoning, and Corporate Social Responsibility is meant to be a practice that addresses them. I will have more to say about these areas later, but for now, it's enough to suggest that business ethics largely stays with philosophy, and the dominant understanding of CSR is as a form of reputational marketing, or a motivational tool for managers to produce happy employees. The idea of strategic CSR, whilst clearly more important than mere CSR, flirts with precisely this idea of 'what we can say about ourselves in order that other people think we are good'. These are subjects used as window dressing in the marketing of the business school, and as a fig leaf in vision statements to cover the conscience of b-school deans. As if talking about ethics and responsibility were the same as doing something about it. They almost never systematically address the simple idea that since current social and economic relations produce the problems that ethics and CSR treat as topics, it is those social and economic relations that need to be changed.

I could go on, but I won't. Most business schools will provide other modules too – in leadership, organizational change, entrepreneurship, advanced topics in accounting and finance, marketing to specialist areas, management in particular sectors, research methods and so on. They will also sometimes provide modules on green business, or critical perspectives on management, or gender and organization, but these latter ones are not common, and almost never core subjects. Their marginal existence can be taken to show the dominance of the areas that I have spent some time describing. It's fair to say that most teaching and research in the majority of business schools across the world would fall into these eleven categories.

CONCEALING CAPITALISM AS COMMON SENSE

You might well think that each of these areas of research and teaching are innocuous enough in themselves, and collectively they just appear to cover all the different dimensions of business activity – money, people, technology, transport, selling and so on. Indeed, the separations between these areas are one of the ways in which they maintain themselves as distinct academic subjects, with different journals, prizes and associations. In this sense, the business and management curriculum is no different from any other part of the university, divided into tribes and territories which guard their fields jealously.

It's an irony then that, despite all the energy put into distinguishing these areas, that they actually share so much, largely because they collectively question so little. The shouty branding which insists that each and every b-school is different and special conceals the fact that most of them are pretty much the same. Subject to the same pressures and markets, they respond with courses and strategies that are effectively identical.[3] The pressure to be like everyone else means that, unlike most social science subjects taught at universities, there is very little attempt to reflect on the practices that they proclaim expertise in. Indeed, much of the 'knowledge' provided is just banality dressed up in tinsel, hyperbolically justified as being relevant and vital with insane statements such as 'Much of what is known in the business arena is obsolete in eighteen months or less.'[4] This is largely to say that they are uncritical in any very meaningful sense. If criticism is mentioned, it would largely be in the academic sense of normal science, being critical of someone else's model or theory. This is a practice which largely ignores the woods for the trees, and which few outside the academy would have any interest in. This is scholastic critique, of counting angels on pinheads, of fine distinctions and extensive literature reviews. It's all kicking off in the lecture theatre, but you can't hear any noise from outside.

The first thing that all these areas share is a powerful sense that the direction of travel of market managerial forms of social order is desirable. It would of course be acknowledged – probably in the opening sentence of the mission statement – that business needs to be more sustainable, diverse and responsible to 'meet the challenges of the future' (or something like that), but the acceleration of global trade, the use of market mechanisms and managerial techniques, the extension of technologies such as accounting, finance and operations are not routinely questioned. This is a progressive account of the modern world, one that relies on the promise of technology, choice, plenty and wealth. Within the business school, capitalism is assumed to be the end of history, an economic model which has trumped all the others, and is now taught as science, rather than ideology.

The second I have already mentioned. This is the assumption that human behaviour – of employees, customers, managers and so on – is best understood as if we are all rational egoists. This provides a set of background assumptions which allow for the development of models of how human beings might be managed in the interests of the business organization. Motivating employees, correcting market failures, designing lean management systems or persuading consumers to spend money are all instances of the same sort of problem. The foregrounded interest here is that of the person who wants control, and the people who are the objects of that interest can then be treated as people who can be manipulated. The task of the manager is to structure the incentives and disincentives in such a way that the individual – because that is the salient unit of behaviour modification – will decide to do this rather than that. Even concepts which appear to imply different foundational assumptions about the nature of human beings – such as culture and community – can be harnessed to this view by being reduced to symbolic or collective structures of incentive which can also be engineered to produce predictable behaviours.

The final similarity I want to point to concerns the nature of the knowledge being produced and disseminated by the business school itself. Because it borrows the gown and mortar board of the university, and cloaks its knowledge in the apparatus of science – journals, professors, big words – it is relatively easy to imagine that the business school is in search of knowledge. This means that the business school very often appears to imagine itself in some rather self-congratulatory ways. This might involve invoking the idea of the university, the neutrality of science, or a conception of public service. The institutional location of the school means that it can employ certain narratives which make the knowledge it sells and the way that it sells it somehow less vulgar and stupid than it really is. Or perhaps this is just the sort of story that lots of organizations tell about themselves, clothing self-interest and a measure of self-disgust in grand talk of corporate social responsibility. And when the trumpets are sounding and the red carpet is rolled out, and the feast is waiting for all the loyal servants, who is going to be stupid enough to suggest that the king has no clothes?

KNOWING FOR WHO?

The business school, as it solidifies and becomes a distinctive place concerned with its own continuation, has tended to become somewhere that produces knowledge *for* management rather than knowledge *about* management. As the professional assemblage hardens, so does it tend to exclude ideas and practices that do not fit easily into the classification systems that have been established. If a form of knowledge cannot be emplaced (perhaps because it is critical of the established order), then, like a misplaced book in a library, it ceases to become useful knowledge and instead falls between the cracks. It becomes unthinkable. The knowledge which is hegemonic in the business school is that which assumes hierarchical organization, market-based forms of exchange (including a marketizing state) and the need for 'management', as occupational group, academic discipline, and practical skill. It is knowledge about how to make capitalism and markets work and that relies on flattering those in power, just as Thomas Bodley did four centuries previously. So the inhabitants of the business school teach about 'leadership' as if it were a form of grace, and host lectures from the rich and powerful, perhaps in the hope that some of their gold might pay for the chicken dinner.

Academic knowledge is made by institutions, and the overall story I have suggested here is one that could be echoed in the rise of any discipline in the last four hundred years. Such assemblages allow us to do all sorts of interesting things, things that would be much more difficult without the supports and scaffolds of the discipline, but we also need to be aware of the constraints that this produces. The b-school makes things possible, but quietly makes other things difficult, too. 'Discipline' can be defined in at least three ways: as a form of training which involves following rules, as an activity that improves a skill, and also as a form of punishment which corrects inappropriate behaviour. None of these are contradictory, because if you want to learn something, you must also learn what *not* to do, and what practices or habits to avoid. This means that certain methods, authorities and evidence themselves become constitutive of what it means to practice a certain discipline, the hidden curriculum, right there in the open, and effectively invisible because it is never contrasted to any other form of knowledge.

Now, in terms of the concerns of this book, this means that the sorts of things that go on in the 'Harvard-style' lecture theatre must be shaped to fit the assumptions of the business school if they are to be recognizable. The materials and practices that are admitted tend to cohere with the dominant assumptions of the school, and the materials and practices that can't be easily co-opted tend to be pushed away, silenced. That is what all the divisions within the university do, not just the business school. Doors are there to keep people out too.

In the next chapter I will consider that which the b-school sells, as well as that which it produces – 'management' as a cadre, practice and academic discipline. Who is the manager, where did they come from and what do they do?

3
What's wrong with management?

As I suggested in Chapter 1, criticisms of management are quite common, even criticisms from within the business school. However, the enemy of my enemy is not necessarily my friend, so this chapter is an attempt to be rather precise about the sort of criticism of management that interests me. This is important, because the logic of the changes to the business school that I will propose depend on a very specific criticism of management, not merely a general grumble about moderately intelligent monkeys in suits. My complaint relates to the way that the hidden curriculum justifies a concentration of power and naturalizes a particular set of economic and social relations.

I begin by assuming that power is always contested. Slave rebellions, peasant revolts and mass revolutions are not merely interruptions to history, but a continual counter-point to all and any concentration of authority. This chapter is concerned with a modern version of power, and a modern version of resistance. Managerialism, as I will define it here, is a relatively recent invention,[1] and it is important to begin by suggesting that it partly emerges as a scientific and meritocratic response to feudal concentrations of inherited power. For many nineteenth-century authors, and the French founders of the business school, the idea of expert organizers was a profoundly radical one. It was an idea that transcended the distinction between capital and labour, and promised to end some older struggles altogether. For the utopian Saint-Simon, for example, the dream of an organized technocracy was constitutive of social progress, of a new order that swept away old despotisms. Yet, even before Saint-Simon, other Frenchmen such as Vincent de Gournay had suggested that 'bureaumania' was in danger of giving petty clerks too much power, and stifling the proper exercise of enterprise. Even before its invention, managerialism was provoking discontent.

As management strengthened its grip during the twentieth century, so did the criticisms become more ubiquitous and noisy. Indeed, in most of popular culture (from the cartoon boss to the mad CEO), we find a portrayal of managers as stupid, selfish, evil, conspiratory and so on. These popular images echo some more fully articulated complaints. From the right, often the attack has been that the managerialists and modernizing technocrats failed to understand the cultural distinctions that were central to legitimizing a divided society with low social mobility. They do not, in other words, know their station. From the point of view of those on the left, the technocrats operate on behalf of the powerful, hiding class interests in their rhetoric about impartiality and markets. They do not, in other words, tell the truth about who they are working for. Rather more bizarrely though, we can now also see managerialism as under attack by consultants and academics who claim that doing business within global e-capitalism means that management (being here a synonym for grey bureaucracy) is too slow and too hierarchical to actually manage very well. The entrepreneurial facilitator of networks demands that the manager gives up the key to their private toilet. Finally, in the most radical critique of all, there is a lengthy tradition of anti-authoritarian positions that could be broadly characterized as anarchist, workerist, feminist and environmentalist. All these positions add up to a trenchant attack on hierarchy and expertise, and demand the end of the manager, but it is the last one that interests me most.

In this chapter, I will explore these portrayals of management over the past 250 years or so. Whilst I certainly don't want to reduce 250 years of dissent, resistance and activism to four boxes, I intend to make two main points. First, managerialism has been under continual attack throughout the modern period, and contemporary forms of criticism are hence articulating some elderly themes. I find this disquieting, since many contemporary academic critiques of managerialism don't seem to be very aware of their historical location, and perhaps of possible connections they might draw with other ideas and traditions. Second, many critiques of managerialism end up (inadvertently I suspect) being rather conservative about the possibilities for alternative forms of organization. Not all of them though, since the more anti-authoritarian varieties appear to open the possibility that the 'manager' might be a temporary character on the historical stage. And this, I will suggest later, is a possibility that is well worth exploring.

THE RELIGION OF NEWTON

Marie-Jean-Antoine-Nicholas de Caritat, Marquis de Condorcet (1743–94) was a supporter of the French Revolution who proposed a highly influential theory of human progress in ten stages, relying heavily on ideas about the usefulness of reason, invention and science. Written whilst in hiding, Condorcet's posthumously published *Sketch for a Historical Picture of the Progress of the Human Spirit* (1795) suggested that the revolution had inaugurated the tenth age of humankind. This would be a golden age in which state education was central to ensuring absolute equality of opportunity and gradual eugenic and health improvements. He supported the emancipation of women, civil marriages, divorce and birth control, and felt that the advanced application of social statistics would be able to guarantee effective pension and insurance systems. His New World would have no wars, and a universal language would help communication and speed intellectual development. He died at the hands of his fellow revolutionary Robespierre, on account of his aristocratic background.

Claude-Henri de Rouvroy, Comte de Saint-Simon was also born into an ancient aristocratic family in Paris in 1760. Saint-Simon refused communion at the age of 13, was imprisoned and then escaped. He acted as an officer on the American side during the American Revolution, fought at the battle of Yorktown, and was again imprisoned. During the French Revolution, despite renouncing his title, he was imprisoned for a while, and spent the rest of the time speculating in land in order to develop a fortune to support his various grand projects (which included what is now the Panama Canal). It was said that his valet had orders to wake him with the phrase, 'Remember, monsieur le Comte, that you have great things to do.' By his 40s, he had squandered his fortune, and began to write, though gaining little attention until a few years before his death in 1825.

What society needed, he thought, was a new stable social order in which the chiefs of industry would control society. These men of science, by virtue of their intelligence and training in philosophy, science and engineering, would be able to rule with the best interests of everyone in mind. Saint-Simon suggested a progressive development towards larger units of 'association' and away from 'subjection'. This 'spontaneous harmony' would be a result of industrialism, and could even result in a European state with homogenous institutions. Though his writings are confused, in *Du Système Industriel* (1821) and *Catéchisme des Industriels* (1824), he puts forward a meritocratic hierarchy in which science is used to produce things which are useful for all. New institutions, such as the chambers of 'Invention', 'Examination' and 'Execution' would organize public works and festivals. Politics would disappear, and become a branch of economics since efficiency and production would be all that mattered in the new order. It doesn't seem any coincidence that the earliest business school was being established in France at the same time.

After his death, several of his disciples (particularly Barthelemy-Prosper Enfantin and Saint-Amand Bazard) established a short-lived journal (*Le Producteur*) and attempted some experiments in communal living, incorporating radical ideas about 'free love' and the equality of the sexes. But it was Saint-Simon's collaboration with Auguste Comte on the journal *L'Organisateur* beginning in 1819 that was crucial in developing his reputation more generally, since Comte's rather mystical faith in science and progress almost entirely echoed Saint-Simon's and Condorcet's ideas. Saint-Simon is perhaps best seen as the grandfather of management,[2] and his faith in a technocratic elite finds clear echoes in later organized utopias, as well as ideas about the importance of the welfare state, administration and bureaucracy. Saint-Simon was certainly a radical, and hostile to inherited privilege, but his radicalism was of a particular kind. Science, being a firm and certain kind of knowledge, a 'religion of Newton' or 'cult of Reason', essentially would play the key role in social engineering. Science, through its elite of experts, would 'shift the Earthly Paradise and transport it from the past into the future'.

GOVERNMENT FROM DESKS

One element of early managerialism is precisely this radical commitment to reorganizing the world more 'scientifically', but it is also difficult to disentangle it from an earlier word: 'bureaucracy'. *Bureaucratie*, rule from the desk, was coined by Vincent de Gournay (1712–59) at least a century before Saint-Simon was born. De Gournay was one of the progressive French 'physiocrats' or 'economists' who stressed a dynamic view of the circulation of wealth against centralized state protectionism. He was, in other words, keen on freeing up the hidden hand of the market, and allowing merchants and the bourgeoisie freedom to make their money, and trickle down wealth to the poor. For de Gournay, *Bureaucratie* was a form of governance by officials which protected state interests, an 'illness', an impediment to the proper exercise of commercial freedoms. As the word moved across Europe, it took with it this connotation of interference, of meddling in things that are best left alone. In 1830s England, the term was often used in resistance to the centralization of poor relief and public health measures. Thomas Carlyle, in 1850, referred to it as 'the continental nuisance' and John Stuart Mill, in 1860, as an inadequate alternative to democracy within which 'the work of government has been in the hands of governors by profession.'

At the turn of the twentieth century, the social theorist who partially rescued bureaucracy from this hostility is undoubtedly Max Weber, who saw the advance of bureaucratization as inevitable, but tied it to a larger sociological thesis about the development of forms of legitimacy. He argued that, in every sphere of social life, from music to war, charismatic and traditional forms of authority are increasingly routinized into legal-rational, or bureaucratic, authority. But Weber's ambivalence about the advance of bureaucracy is clear. On the one hand, he lists its advantages:

> The fully developed bureaucratic mechanism compares with other organisations exactly as does the machine with the non-mechanical modes of production.
> Precision, speed, unambiguity, knowledge of the files, continuity, discretion, unity, strict subordination, reduction of friction and of material and personal costs – these are raised to the optimum point ....

Yet he is also painfully aware of its consequences:

> Its specific nature, which is welcomed by capitalism, develops the more perfectly the more bureaucracy is 'dehumanised',

the more completely it succeeds in eliminating from official business love, hatred and all purely personal, irrational, and emotional elements which escape calculation ... the professional bureaucrat is chained to his activity by his entire material and ideal existence. In the great majority of cases, he is only a single cog in an ever-moving mechanism which prescribes to him an essentially fixed route of march.[3]

Weber's ambivalence echoes through the twentieth century. Harold Laski, in 1930, defines bureaucracy as 'a system of government the control of which is so completely in the hands of officials that their power jeopardises the liberties of ordinary citizens'. In 1950, Harold Lasswell and Abraham Kaplan refer to it as 'the form of rule in which the élite is composed of officials'. Indeed, much of US sociology and psychology after the Second World War was concerned with various ways in which the authoritarian Fascist or Communist versions of bureaucracy could be better understood and avoided. Descriptions of authoritarian personality types, experiments on the willingness of subjects to obey people in white coats, groupthink and conformity, and accounts of the dysfunctions of bureaucracy abound. The more perceptive of these commentators, such as Hannah Arendt, suggest that we all use Eichmann's excuse that he 'was merely following orders'.

In his celebrated book, *The Organization Man*, William Whyte describes the 'social ethic' (which 'could be called an organisation ethic, or a bureaucratic ethic') as a pervasive form of dull conformity. For Whyte, this is a climate that 'inhibits individual initiative and imagination, and the courage to exercise it against group opinion'. Around the same time, Herbert Marcuse (who cites Whyte approvingly) characterized modern societies as 'one dimensional' in the sense that people at work, and in their leisure, were becoming mere instruments for the mechanical organization of capitalism, while situationists like Debord launched an assault on a culture based on 'time-which-is-money', submission to bosses, boredom, exhaustion … The organisation of work and the organisation of leisure are the blades of the castrating shears whose job is to improve the race of fawning dogs.'

More lately, and more carefully, both Alisdair MacIntyre and Zygmunt Bauman have complained that management and bureaucracy are narrowing human sensitivities. For different reasons, both these authors end up arguing that the calculating human is replacing the feeling human. They take aim at instrumental forms of utilitarianism which efface the possibility of asking more general questions about values and ethics because a boundary is constructed between personal convictions and organizational duty.[4]

One of the most pervasive things about this diagnosis of 'government from desks' is the idea that bureaucracy somehow restricts agency. In an echo of Rousseau, free people are constrained, whether they be the bureaucrats or their clients, the victims of Fascism or the victims of Stalinism, the executives or their customers. De Gournay might have felt that the constraint was primarily a commercial one, whilst Bauman felt it was a moral one, but the linking theme is that bureaucracy stops us from doing things. It places red tape around our throats, and ties us to desks.

FOUR FORMS OF DISCONTENT

The word 'bureaucracy' does not mean the same as the word 'management', but they are certainly very overlapping concepts. Management, in an etymological and common-sense way, also has some connotation of being led by the nose – one of its origins being the handling of horses – and that sense of constraint certainly informs its critics. Yet there are some very different complaints about managerialism, both in terms of explaining what it is, and what we should do about. Hence if we want to understand what it means to be critical of management, we need to acknowledge its rather complex history. From de Gournay to the present day, there are a variety of positions, and a variety of forms of discontent. In other words, lots of people don't like management, but their reasons differ considerably. Within Critical Management Studies, many authors have worried a lot about what the word 'critical' means. In order that the boundary between 'us' and 'them' is clear, it is necessary to distinguish between the sort of critique that is morally righteous and that which is self-interested posturing. The problem is that there are lots of people who claim to be critical of the current climate of managerialism: business ethicists, opportunistic management gurus, relativizing postmodernists, consumer champions, doctrinaire Marxists, careful reformers and the sort of people who throw bricks through McDonald's' windows. But these people do not themselves agree on the distribution of the righteous and the self-interested. Indeed, they actually agree about very little.

For example, if we take many state leftist critiques of management, it is usually the case that the central target is not management as a specific way of thinking about authority relations and expertise, but rather as a representative for the interests of capitalists. In that sense, Marx, Lenin, Mao, Guevara and so on were rarely directly concerned with alternatives to technocratic governance. Either the assumption is made that the post-revolutionary leader will embody the 'real' interests of the governed, or that (at some unspecified point) the institutions of the state and of capital, will wither away to be replaced by a decentralized system of worker organizations. The former ends up with Lenin's enthusiasm for Taylorism, and the latter was actively resisted by those in power in Moscow, Havana and Beijing. Quite clearly, not all state communists are against management, even though they might have something to say about ownership. So, if we disregard what I think are basically authoritarian critiques of authoritarianism, we are left with a variety of positions that actually engage with management and managerialism per se. I will divide this section into four parts, which broadly cover complaints rooted in nostalgia, modernization, everyday cultural experience, and (most importantly, for my purposes) anti-authoritarianism.

Nostalgic critique

Consider Protherough and Pick's *Managing Britannia* from 2002, an exploration of the culture of managerialism in Blair's Britain. The authors seem to detest much about the age that they live in, and they believe that 'management' is the problem. Theirs is the sort of conservatism that rails against 'bureaumania' in the name of personal freedoms. Management is a bad thing because it is an extension of the petty mentality of the *petit bourgeois* once they move into positions of responsibility and power. The state has mutated into a sprawling apparatus based around the idea that everything must be controlled. Government becomes a gigantic nosy neighbour, and no Englishman can now claim that his home is still his castle. Protherough and Pick seem to believe that the past was a lot better – when the local baker made wholesome bread and good administrators displayed wholesome traits of personal character. And then the world started to change for the worse. This, I think, is a form of anti-managerialism that has some ancient ancestors and some rather conservative implications.

Indeed, many cultural nostalgics, from John Ruskin and William Morris to Matthew Arnold and T.S. Eliot seem to have equated cultural decline with bureaucratization and commerce. More recently, George Ritzer has replayed this attitude with a Weberian spin in his celebrated 'McDonaldization' thesis.[5] It seems to me that Protherough and Pick's attempt to rescue culture from the 'robotic grasp of the bureaucrats' exemplifies this long-standing theme. This is the nostalgic liberalism of 'intellectuals' who fear that commerce and mass administration are replacing warm human values. To be clear here, Protherough and Pick are not anarcho-libertarians in the sense that they wish to argue against any and all forms of intervention. They seem happy enough for the state to exist, and for organizations to do whatever it is that they do. What seems to annoy them most is that *certain* forms of culture and language are being degraded by the shrill demand for key performance indicators. They spend almost no time worrying about the call centre, but vent a great deal of spleen against those who have tried to claim that universities, art galleries, theatres, churches and culture itself should be subjected to the same kind of intrusive controls. This is an aesthetic judgement of the 'how dare they!' variety. It is the crassness and vulgarity of these jumped-up traffic wardens with MBAs that seems to annoy them most, and the 'deadening' effects of managerial language that provide their most common illustrations.[6]

Protherough and Pick's is a kind of anti-modern critique, one engaged in the lengthy class-inflected debate between conservatives and reforming utilitarians. Though they are never explicit about what they *do* want to sponsor (being happier bashing everyone else), they seem to have a faith in the intrinsic qualities of a particular form of life, a romanticized version of occupation as vocation. They complain that 'the British worker is no longer a craftsman or professional, but has been forced into acting as a state controlled automaton.'[7] Working-class struggle against capitalist deskilling in the workplace, and the self-interested market strategies of highly paid elites, are reduced to a lost idyll of happy industrial feudalism. What Protherough and Pick want is 'proper, old fashioned management' which pits 'common sense' against the halogen brightness of nasty 'modern' management.

So management here stands for a series of connected elements of modern life: urbanization, rationalization, the division of labour and social mobility. For many European writers, management often also means something rather brash, brutal and North

American. It is important to note that conservative and radical nostalgic critiques can end up in rather similar places, with Ruskin's and Morris's hostility to industrialism chiming with craft and guild ideas from a romanticized pre-capitalist economy. The accountant, the buzz word and the business school become emblems of cultural decline and we wait for the return of the local, the authentic and the re-establishment of legitimate authority. Probably the most important element in this nostalgic critique is this last one. It is not a question of the refusal of hierarchy in itself, but rather the insistence that modern hierarchies are based on vulgar or incorrect criteria. This is not a denial of leadership, but an insistence that we are currently being led by the wrong people. Managers need to be put back in their place.

Modernising critique

In precisely the place that we might expect to find a certain defensiveness about attacks on management, we also find that some modernizing radicals are against it too. With the growth of state and corporate administrations throughout the twentieth century, the new De Gournays wish to once again claim that there is not enough enterprise going on anymore. Consultants can describe themselves as 'revolutionaries', and claim to be hostile to the sclerotic effects of management as a new kind of 'bureaumania'. In much of the First World, the 1960s saw the beginnings of a long attempt to articulate administration as solid and inflexible compared to fast-moving 'organic' organizations that would be able to survive in a hyper-global market. Futurologists could claim that an older world was sliding away, and that the new post-whatever times needed to be post-bureaucratic too. Consultants could sell ideas about culture (not structure), re-engineering (not incrementalism), and spirit (not loyalty). A decentralized network was talked into being, and dot-coms replaced automobile companies as the exemplars of a new age.

In its most contemporary form then, management has now become another word for dull grey administration, and has been replaced by 'leadership' or, even better, 'transformational leadership'. The charismatic leader returns, slashing bravely through the thickets of departments and memoranda. Being against management means being for the customer, understanding the market, being able to change strategy rapidly and so on. In terms of organizational structure, dinosaurs are to be divided into smaller and more focused units. In terms of individual psychology, the winners are the innovators, the non-conformists, the 'intra-preneurs'. Add to this the Internet, and you can produce something that looks like a anti-organizational manifesto, but one that says very little about capitalism, ownership, profit and so on. Authors such as Thomas Frank have nicely demonstrated how easily this patina of radicalism can be grafted on to what Frank calls 'market populism'. In other words, it is the fault of management that public services don't work well, or that commercial organizations can't satisfy our every whim. We must ditch hierarchy and embrace whatever neologism is proposed as a critique of the present and a solution for the future.[8] This is airport bookstall radicalism, assuming that Amazon doesn't end up closing those down too. It is also a form of radicalism that is easily reproduced and sold by the business school itself, with Che and the skull-and-cross-bones decorating capitalism 2.0.

Cultural critique

The two forms of engagement above are both, more or less, 'political' with a big P, in the sense that they clearly and deliberately engage in a criticism of the language, strategy and character of management. Yet these ideas are also more ordinary, part of the common culture that surrounds the Global North, and that surrounds the business school too.

An advert for delivery company Fedex features a young man on his first day at work. His boss points at a pile of parcels and says:

'We're in a bit of a jam. All this stuff has to get out today.'
'Yeah, er ... I don't do despatch.'
'Oh no, no, it's very easy, we use Fedex. Anybody can do it.'
'You don't understand. I have an MBA.'
'Oh, you have an MBA?'
'Yeah ...'
'In that case, I'll have to show you how to do it.'[9]

Whether we are considering film, TV, comic books, advertising or the Internet, this is a ubiquitous form of criticism, a sort of hidden curriculum of popular culture.[10] In workplaces, we find noticeboards containing multiply photocopied witticisms about the nature of work; spam emails have attachments that pretend to be a powerpoint from the boss; MBA students and their teachers read Dilbert, and small *Books of Management Bollocks* are for sale in gift shops. Websites and blogs offer ways of getting back at your boss, often using extreme violence, and tales of cubicle slavery are documented in the imagined freedom of cyberspace. On the small screen, bosses and management are endlessly lampooned in situation comedies. Over-promoted, power-crazed dumbwits parade their insecurities in front of sarcastic employees. And, since the 1970s, contemporary films, whether realist or fantastic, have managers in the role that would traditionally have been played by the mafia mobster, or the cowboy in the black hat. Blockbusters as varied as *Spiderman*, *Bridget Jones' Diary* and *Monsters Inc.* all have plots that revolve around managerial conspiracies. Sometimes this is explicitly thematized, as in films like *You've Got Mail* or *Disclosure*, sometimes it is a feature of the back story that allows us to easily understand why the bad guy is bad, as in the *Robocop* films or *Mission Impossible 2*. Indeed, I would argue that almost the only place you can find a representation of a good manager in English-speaking culture nowadays is in the b-school penumbra of consultants, textbooks and training courses.

Yet, as with other forms of anti-managerialism, this is not new. In a strong stream of quasi-gothic imagery, the cultural critique of managerialism goes much further back than this. In Dickens, Zola, Gaskell and other industrial commentators of the mid-nineteenth century, we find a series of complaints about the character of the manager, of the emergence of bureaumania and the soaring hierarchies of organizations. Even Gilbert and Sullivan, in their 1893 operetta *Utopia Unlimited*, gently parodied the bright-eyed optimism of people who believed that joint stock companies would solve all their problems. The turn of the twentieth century and the rise of robber baron capitalism articulated discontent in much more powerful ways. The Czech dramatist Karel Capek introduced the word 'robot' into English through his 1922 play *R.U.R* – 'Rossum's Universal Robots'. In the play, the robots (from the Czech *robota* meaning drudgery, with connotations of serfdom) are manufactured by a company as 'living machines' without souls. Of course, at that time – immediately after the 'Great' War – Taylor, Bedeaux, Gantt, Gilbreth and so on were suggesting that it really was possible to control employees in increasingly machinic detail. Within the organization, aliens with little English, such as Frederick Taylor's 'dumb ox' Schmidt, were being disciplined, shaped and moulded before they could become useful.

Like the robotic workers in films such as *Metropolis* (1926) and *A Nous La Liberté* (1932) and Charlie Chaplin's defiant little tramp in *Modern Times* (1936), these humans become part of factory or office machines – black-and-white characters marching to the timings of the machine whilst their bosses smoke big cigars upstairs. Franz Kafka's books *The Trial* (1925) and *The Castle* (1926) capture a more general sense of these organizational nightmares. Within their labyrinths of mysterious conspiracies, helpless individuals endlessly attempt to understand the reasons for their circumstances, and bureaucrats defer to rulebooks and superiors that are nowhere to be found. These concerns with rationalization and hierarchy are nicely echoed in Aldous Huxley's 1932 *Brave New World*. Set in the World State's Western European Zone, Huxley named his 'Fordship' the Controller Mustapha Mond, after Sir Alfred Mond, the first chairman of Imperial Chemical Industries. The key problem for this dystopia, as in Yevgeny Zamyatin's explicitly Taylorist 'OneState' of *We* (1924) or Orwell's later *1984* (1948), is how the individual can resist the anti-human bureaucracy that wishes to practice what Huxley prophetically called 'Human Element Management'.

In the US context, there had also been growing suspicion of increasing corporate power from the beginning of the century onwards. Ambrose Bierce, in his *Devil's Dictionary* of 1911, defined the corporation as 'An ingenious device for obtaining individual profit without individual responsibility'.[11] The organization of the US economy under the control of the so-called 'trusts' ensured that prices were set in smoke-filled rooms and profits guaranteed. Yet, after the First World War, the Great Depression, the stock market crash, muckraking journalism, substantial attempts at union organization by the IWW and the CIO together with violent resistance by industrialists, all turned this sense of unease into widespread social concern. The rise of the Progressive Party and the 'trustbusters' was in some sense a response to the widespread sense of corruption and collusion, and the perception that both big business and big politics were effectively in each other's pockets.

The brave promise of an America of social opportunity now sees the 'little guy' suffering under the new yoke of big organization. Social commentary books such as Matthew Josephson's *The Robber Barons* (1934), Frederick Lewis Allen's

The Lords of Creation (1935) and Thurman Arnold's *The Folklore of Capitalism* (1937) all took aim at the new, decadent American aristocracy.

> In short order the railroad presidents, the copper barons, the big dry-goods merchants and the steel masters became Senators, ruling in the highest councils of the national government, and sometimes scattered twenty-dollar gold pieces to the newsboys of Washington. But they also became in even greater number lay leaders of churches, trustees of universities, partners or owners of newspapers or press services and figures of fashionable, cultured society.[12]

There was a widespread hostility in the US to the rich in their skyscrapers, the con-artists on Wall Street and their stooges in the government. Films like *Mr Smith Goes to Washington* (1939), and *It's a Wonderful Life* (1946) are centrally organized around a dichotomy between the little guy and the bad politician or financier. In the latter, George Bailey, the long-suffering owner of Bailey Savings and Loan, prevents the town of Bedford Falls from falling into the clutches of the evil Mr Potter and his big bank. This narrative of community and common virtue versus big business was certainly the most common mythical subtext in the US, whilst in Europe these concerns seemed to focus more on bureaucratic rationalization and the simultaneous rise of worker's associations and socialist politics. On both sides of the Atlantic, management was getting a bad press.

Whether Gradgrind in Dickens' *Hard Times*, or David Brent and Michael Scott in the TV sitcom *The Office*, cultural discontent about managerialism often has diffuse targets. Since there is no definitive 'reading' of any cultural text, it would be difficult to decide whether the precise 'against' was the business school, management, rationalization, capitalism or work itself. Nonetheless, the figure of the manager is central here. Whether demonic and conspiratorial, or ridiculous and self-obsessed, the point is that they are a culturally troubling figure. They appear to represent a power with the potential for great evil and coercion, a power with a legitimacy that is highly questionable, or even with the hint of illegitimacy concerning their social mobility.[13] Whether cultural discontent is the same as dissent, or even resistance, is not the issue here. This critique in culture clearly doesn't have a great deal of effect, because b-schools are thriving and the number of managers continues to grow, but it clearly shows that the virtues of management are routinely challenged. If we add in the nostalgic or modernizing complaints I have already addressed above, then we appear to have a variety of positions from which the very idea of 'management' is being consistently attacked, and that is before we even start to think about the serious alternatives.

Anti-authoritarian critique

Before the words 'management' and 'bureaucracy' had been coined, there were slaves and masters, ecclesiastical hierarchies, patriarchal and ethnic hierarchies, imperial states, feudal structures of land ownership, and the East India Company. There were also Amazons, Cathars, Diggers, Levellers and Dissenters. My point is that dissent to managerialism is one small element of dissent aimed at all sorts of other sorts of authority relations. Once again, it is well worth re-emphasizing that versions of managerial rationalization were often enough seen as a radical improvement to the capricious power of kings. From Thomas More's original 1516 *Utopia* onwards, a consistent theme in Western utopianism has been the well-ordered city-state. In works such as Campanella's *City of the Sun* (1602), Etienne Cabet's *Voyage to Icaria* (1839), or Edward Bellamy's *Looking Backward* (1888), the managerial meritocracy is very clear, and it is a form of order that anticipates Weber's description of bureaucracy.

Yet these autocratic utopias also have their counterpoint in a utopianism and politics that rejects hierarchy, and treats issues of organization and order as potentially distributable across a community that is organized differently. William Morris's novel *News from Nowhere* (1890) is, in part, a reaction to Bellamy's *Looking Backward*. Where Bellamy was lauding a technologically sophisticated version of strong state socialism, Morris is describing an arcadia of small market towns in which production and ownership are communal. Morris wants work to be desired, to be a natural part of the human condition. People gather together in 'banded workshops' to enjoy the exercise of their craft, but there is no compulsion to work. Such compulsion would simply produce ugly objects, and debased people. *News from Nowhere* can easily be read as an anarchist eco-topia, set in a future that is producing a new kind of people, freed from relations of slavery and repression.

In that sense, the key set of thinkers who should be considered as early anti-managerialists are those generally associated with anarchisms of various kinds. Anarchism is organization theory in the truest sense, a theory that takes nothing about human beings and their organizational capacities for granted. Rather than assuming, as many more conservative organizational theorists do, the existence of the division of labour, capitalism, hierarchy and so on, all these 'facts' become questions. No 'natural order' is assumed, and issues of governance, control, decision making, production and so on are all assumed to be matters that the autonomous individual and collective can make intelligent choices about. Management, in anything other than the role of a temporary co-ordinating function, is simply superfluous since people can usually organize themselves. More damagingly, management also disempowers, appropriates and dominates. It persuades people that they are too stupid to organize themselves. Unsurprisingly, given that anarchists are not keen on being told what to do, there is little agreement on any other guiding principles. Writers such as Godwin, Stirner, Proudhon, Bakunin, Kropotkin, and Tolstoy rarely suggest similar solutions to similar problems. Some stress forms of association at the local level, others assume that autonomy is a value that should not be compromised by any constraints. Many assume that certain constraints are acceptable in order to maintain a minimal social order, but there would be considerable debate about the nature and force of those agreements. Whatever the view, the privileges of managerialism would certainly be questioned in most forms of anarchist thought.[14]

However, when we move towards the anarcho-syndicalist versions of anarchism, the importance of more elaborate organizational forms becomes apparent. Since the aim of syndicalists is primarily large-scale political change, then the use of industrial action, particularly the general strike, is seen as a means of defending the interests of workers against management and of overthrowing the present order. However, in order to achieve this, labour organizations need to develop the self-governing structures that will form the basis of the subsequent control of production by workers. It is here that more centralized forms of authority might become tolerated for tactical reasons, something that we also see in some co-operatively owned organizations. Nonetheless, syndicalists pursue a long-term strategy that intends to result in forms of workplace democracy and worker self-management.[15]

This leads into the co-operative movement itself, usually based on a form of socialist or collectivist, rather than anarchist, politics. There is a considerable continuum of work and practice here, ranging from forms of minimal involvement and ownership that retain most managerial privileges (such as employee share ownership, and versions of empowerment), co-production and time banking, through to fully fledged co-operative forms of ownership and control. The latter are particularly vibrant today in Italian workerism, Argentinian recuperated factories, the

Mondragon co-operative network and so on. As with anarchism, these ideas are not new, and can be dated back, at least, to the English labour economists, Robert Owen and the Rochdale Pioneers among others. Though forms of management are common enough within these forms of organization, it is rather that the activity of co-ordination is treated as being a functional necessity. Management is not lionized, and often subject to constraints on tenure and pay, as well as being subject to scrutiny by some sort of council of workers or worker representatives.[16] This is management being tolerated, rather than celebrated.

Another current of anti-managerial thought is rather more recent, and is associated with versions of radical and anarcha-feminism. Patriarchy could be seen to be the original form of oppressive authority from which all others grow. Feminists, it is argued, should thus struggle against all forms of hierarchy, and towards ways of being that are more collective and supportive. It could be argued that Emma Goldman was the originator of this simultaneous attack on both liberal feminism and managerial capitalism. However, as with anarchism and workerism, there are many inflections within feminist resistance to authority.[17] Feminists might take their principal problem to be men, leading to separatist forms of organization. Or they might articulate the problem as patriarchal relations, or capitalist relations, or some combination of both. In addition, the intersections between feminism and forms of environmentalism are also particularly strong. However, whatever the emphasis, the general point would be that radical feminists are suspicious about the naturalization of authority, the division of labour, and any separation between public and private action, such as that embodied in a Weberian description of bureaucracy. Man/agers tend to operate without hatred or passion, and in so doing, end up assuming both separation and dominance. Management, as practice and discipline, produces the rational egoist constituted by the social relations of the workplace and described within the discipline of organizational behaviour. Such people do not admit weakness, play with children, or imagine themselves as anything other than selves.

We find a similar diversity of anti-authoritarian positions within green or environmentalist thought. In this case, it is very often the human relationship to nature that is articulated as an original hierarchy, though ecofeminist positions would also argue that this is a peculiarly male way of relating to the natural world. So if positions of dominance and exploitation are problematic, then it is obvious enough that more collective and co-operative relations should be encouraged within our work and our communities. Of crucial importance here is the trend to localization, to the grass roots. As Ernst Schumacher said, small is beautiful, and the sorts of organizational relations sponsored by green activists and writers would tend to be based on ideas of the eco-village, and the sustainable community. Co-ordination may require a limited division of labour, but the general principal would usually be that hierarchy should be minimized, and forms of collective decision making would be the norm. Again, it needs to be noted that there is no 'one' environmental position. Variants of collectivism and individualism, as well as diagnoses of the source of the problem, shade over into feminist, socialist and anarchist positions.[18] Uniting these varieties of radical thought and practice would be metaphors of 'working with' and being 'close to', which would tend to refuse the physical or intellectual separations that managerialism must necessarily rely on.

Anti-authoritarian critiques of managerialism are clearly entangled with a variety of other complaints, but they all share a deep distrust of the notion of the expert organizer. The centrality of the manager, as someone with more status and reward who is not involved in day-to-day organizing, is entirely antithetical to most anarchist, socialist, feminist and environmentalist thinkers. In addition, these ideas are inextricably entangled with actual practices. Whether we look at the long history of intentional communities, co-operatives, alternative economic practices or contemporary attempts to resist the hegemony of the capitalist work organization, these are discontents that produce working alternatives. And these are not temporary, minor, or historical alternatives, but a continual stream of practical opposition that is as vibrant now as it has ever been.

AGAINST MANAGEMENT?

If we take my rapidly sketched picture as a whole, then it is obvious that 'management' (broadly conceived) has always been contested, and from a wide variety of theoretical and political locations. More recently, the business school has come to stand as a lightning rod or symbol for these discontents, but it is part of a long history of complaints about the powers of the technocrat.

At the risk of simplification, let me propose a way of classifying the differences between these grumbles. What I called the *nostalgic* critique is generally aimed from 'above' management, both in terms of social class and claimed moral elevation. It is essentially a 'high cultural' discontent that suggests that management is a debasing force, an example of the way in which modernity corrupts a more authentic authority structure. Very often, the person doing the complaining might well feel that their position or profession is insufficiently respected, and that modernization means increasing marginalization. The *modernizing* critique is different in that it appears to originate from 'alongside' management. It is a form of discontent that seeks to move management over, in order that a new order can occupy its place. This is the voice of a putative 'new generation' of organizers, a group of young princes (and occasionally princesses) inviting their elderly relative to vacate the site of power. The complaint is simply that management could be done better, often just by calling it something else.

By contrast, the *cultural* and *anti-authoritarian* critiques appear to be located 'below' management. In the case of the former, this occurs pretty much by default, since the location of the reader of the cartoon or listeners to the joke is assumed to be someone who shares the assumption that all managers are, by definition, shits who shit on you. Popular culture, in the broadest sense, speaks for the popular, for the people, and hence rarely provides a sympathetic account of the troubles of those with power. Those with power are assumed to be quite capable of doing that for themselves. The second critique from 'below' is rather more nuanced, in that it does attempt to speak for various interests that it claims have not been represented within contemporary market managerialism. Whether articulating the distinctive voices and possibilities of women, workers, nature, community, or the autonomous individual, the general point is that these are proposals (and often experiments) in organizing that are quite self-consciously anti-managerial. They open the possibility that managerialism can be seen as only one form of organizing, and not a synonym for organization in general. However, this is not to say that they all share a common agenda, just that they are generally opposed to similar things. The nature of this opposition means that they all articulate management as a discipline, occupation, or activity which constrains and dis-empowers. Hence words like 'collectivity', 'democracy', and 'autonomy' are likely to be seen as part of a solution.

We shouldn't assume that 'above', 'alongside' and 'below' are incommensurable positions. Perhaps it would be better to describe them as tendencies, since they can be combined in various ways. For example, William Morris appears to combine medieval nostalgia with a proto-communist sensibility and some highly prescient nods towards environmentalism. Radical cyber-libertarians often propose modernization precisely in order that decision making can be distributed, and networks take the place of hierarchies. Cultural critique is not insulated from alternative organization, but can be used self-consciously to pursue explicitly political ends, as in the case of situationism, feminism and autonomism. Finally, anarchists can be nostalgics or modernizers too – it depends on their attitudes to technology, the urban, and the relations between human and 'nature'. In sum, we should not expect that anti-managerial positions will be simple, because managerialism is not simple. It gets inflected differently in different times and places, and hence invites different condemnations. Many anti-management positions are contradictory in their implications, only joined together by a vague common enemy, a sense that the business school teaches people to become cold-hearted bastards.

To conclude this chapter then. It is often enough assumed within the business school that humans are better at organizing things nowadays, and that the rise and rise of the manager reflects the need for professionally trained organizers to deal with more and more complex organization. This chapter has shown that this is a very one-sided history, and that it opens into a future that is eminently contestable. Aside from reflecting the interests and dreams of a powerful occupational ideology, there are all sorts of ways of thinking against management, and there always have been. At the same time that Saint-Simon was writing, across the channel William Blake was opposing the consequences of industrialism: the 'dark satanic mills', slavery and sexual inequality. An anarchist before the word had been coined, he rejected all forms of imposed authority and said 'I must create my own system or be enslaved by another man's.' Just as Saint-Simon was celebrating order, so was Blake viewing society as inevitably restricting the freedoms derived from intuition and spontaneity. He would have been against management too, had he known about it.

In the next chapter, we will move from history to the present, from the general to the specific. This means summarizing what contemporary critics have said about the sort of management that is being taught in the sleek training academies. And who are these contemporary critics? Well, it turns out that most of them (like me) are business school employees. So what are they so exercised about?

4

What's wrong with the business school?

It will no doubt shock the reader considerably if I admit that I was exaggerating a little in Chapter 2, in presenting the business school as if its employees were all smug robots who unthinkingly copy out 'greed is good' onto their interactive whiteboards and then go and check their bank accounts. I apologize. I was being unfair. They aren't all like that. (Though if you do read what many of them write about their places of employment, the amalgam of smugness and stupidity is a little hard to bear.)

Indeed, as I suggested in Chapter 1, quite a lot of the criticism of the business school has come from within the schools themselves. This is an odd thing. Most organizations have their worst enemies outside the building – signing petitions, agitating, demonstrating, perhaps even throwing a brick or two through the window – but the business school employs most of its critics, and keeps paying them, whatever they say about it.[1] No doubt this tells us something about the ineffectual nature of the criticism, and the strength of the institution, but that doesn't mean that the howling should be ignored. Some of the more thoughtful commentators have made a variety of interesting complaints about what they do, and I'm going to say something about those in this chapter. However, it is also important to understand them as variations on the nostalgic and modernizing criticisms of management that I presented in the previous chapter. These are rarely radical diagnoses of how things might be done differently, but tend to be complaints aimed at ameliorating the worst arrogances and stupidities, or soliciting a new form of capitalism which is greener, kinder and more inclusive. As you can guess, I don't think this is enough, but more about that later in the book.

For now, let's begin by reminding ourselves that business and management degrees have become the most popular university qualification across the Global North, so I think we can legitimately assume that these qualifications have consequences for the graduates themselves and the organizations and societies that they inhabit. (After all, if they don't, then the whole thing is a fairy story.) What sort of behaviour do business schools teach? What kind of character do they encourage in those who will be running the organizations that make the modern world? (And bear in mind that the remarkable George W. Bush was the first president to have an MBA, from Harvard in his case.) What would Plato say about this kind of education of our guardians?

CRASH

In the immediate aftermath of the latest (at the time of writing) financial crisis beginning in 2007, there were plenty of people (including me) willing to write op-ed pieces for newspapers on why the business school was to blame.[2] Well, not entirely to blame, because there were a few other institutions involved too, but it was commonly suggested that the business school had laid the groundwork for a certain attitude to commercial activity that was particularly damaging. Such suggestions weren't exclusively a post-crash phenomenon, because plenty of high-status business school employees had been making some pretty trenchant criticisms before then too.[3] The range of those criticisms is broad, ranging from the idea that the curriculum is too academic and not connected to actual management practice, all the way to proposing that the business school really just teaches greed and selfishness. It is also common to point out that key figures in the crash, as well as earlier business scandals such as Enron and WorldCom, had MBAs from good business schools. It is unclear just what the moral of this fun fact is of course. It might be that having an MBA didn't prevent people from engaging in risky or corrupt practices, or that it actually encouraged them. More research is clearly needed.

Often, the preface to the accusation of blame bemoans the fact that business schools have lost trust, that they have (perhaps like many institutions) become seen to be corrupt places, primarily interested in collecting feathers for their own nests. This is described as a crisis of legitimacy, a moment when the established authorities are being questioned, and we are told that it requires a response. Setting aside the idea of a golden age when ordinary people really did trust the b-school (and I wonder what evidence might be provided for that claim), this is a sad lament, and often one that provokes intense reflection by the academics concerned.[4] Is this what they have spent their careers doing? Have all their youthful hopes been betrayed?

The world we have lost

This is a pervasive atmosphere within many of the books and articles in this area, a sense that the promise of the past has not been fulfilled. There are different versions of when the golden age might have existed, but the diagnosis is common. For some, as I mentioned in Chapter 1, the best times were those that began with Joseph Wharton's republican paternalism, and drove the foundation of business schools as places to teach both character and technique. The idea of the grave responsibilities of teaching those who might rule appears to be important in the early pro-nouncements of benefactors and b-school deans and presidents (but then they would say that wouldn't they?). What often comes over is that, in the US case particularly, there is an attempt at a civilizing process. The business school is justified as a form of moral armament against the sins of corruption and greed which were so clearly shaping early twentieth-century robber baron capitalism. So perhaps the business school used to be a force for good, but now?

For US b-school employees like Rakesh Khurana and Ellen O'Connor in their impressive histories of the institution, ideas about professionalism, morality and civic virtues were constitutive of early US schools, but these 'higher aims' have now been degraded into the production of 'hired hands' – obedient servants of large corporations. A slightly different version of this can be found in Mie Augier and James March's version of the business school of the second half of the twentieth century. Following criticisms of the quality of US research and teaching as (in Herbert Simon's words) 'wastelands of vocationalism', a Ford and Carnegie Foundation report of 1959 resulted in a concerted attempt to move business education into the space age. The result was the idea of a school driven by science and decision models, by the firm conviction that society and organizations could be properly governed by technocrats and technology. This was the application of physics envy to public policy, a place which attempted to be value neutral in the service of a wider social good, a university for producing New Deal planners with computers and a sound knowledge of the laws governing human behaviour in groups.[5]

In both accounts, we have some common ideas. The business school was a place that delineated a particular class of people – managers – by equipping them with a form of language and knowledge. It also made business schools the gatekeepers to being defined as one of these people, as well as the generators of the knowledge that they needed to know. In that sense, the technocratic phase of the US business school is really the intensification of the project, but using science rather than morality as its justification. Whenever the golden age, the diagnosis of decline from the 1970s onwards is pretty much the same though.

For Augier and March, the counter-culture of the '60s lays the foundation for the 'triumph of the self' of the 1970s and onwards, by which they seem to mean the triumph of selfishness. Ideas about collective action are in decline, and hence so was the serious research needed to make intelligent collective choices. Behind this, of course, was the rise of finance, the tides of money and algorithms that made selling and buying companies and cash a more profitable endeavour than actually making things.

The wolves of Wall Street

Part of this nostalgic diagnosis is that finance, economics, statistics and operations research has become dominant within the business school, reflecting the wider dominance of neoliberal accounts of people and markets. This is the business school as imagined by a trader in stocks and shares, resting on neoclassical ideas about economic man and understanding ethics and politics as market imperfections.

Within the business school, this means that the dominant explanation for the phenomenon of 'management' has become the idea that 'managers' are the agents of those who own the capital. Since people generally can't be trusted because they are oriented to self-maximizing behaviours, managers can't really be trusted either, so they have to be bribed with lots of cash and stock options in order to act in a way that benefits the share price. Resting on this theory, business strategy becomes understood as an attempt to maximize share prices. Finance becomes understood as the alchemy of business, turning the world into gold, and its magic is increasingly applied to all actual, potential and virtual assets. The market is imagined a way of thinking about the past, present and future, and its prices are treated as if they were signals from the gods, in a way that exemplifies a kind of collective madness. There is almost no consideration of the irrational exuberance which creates bubbles, of systematic market imperfections, of regulation and its politics both by the state and by companies themselves.

In a brilliant essay written in 2005, London Business School professor Sumantra Ghoshal condemned these 'ideologically inspired amoral theories'.[6] He saw these theories as self-fulfilling prophecies which encouraged pessimism about human behaviour, and management behaviour in particular. In fact, he says, management's world-view produces situations which lead to the opportunism and short-term behaviour that Ghoshal describes. Unlike physics, this faux-physics of people has consequences. Responsibility for the moral, political and ethical is avoided, often passed off to somewhere else – to the shareholders, to the system, to external forces, to human nature itself. Ghoshal sees this as the reduction of the complex problems of balancing the needs of employees, managers, and shareholders to a mathematical problem of distribution to the shareholders. This is bad theory, he says, in that it doesn't actually explain what happens, and it has bad consequences, in that it produces bad people.

Liberalism, and art

The answer, Ghoshal suggests, is that the curriculum needs to be rebalanced and become 'pluralist', it needs to be returned to a time before finance became quite so dominant. He calls this 'pluralism', and seems to be referring to a liberal arts model of character formation, pretty much a reinvention of what the early US schools said about themselves. This is a call which has been taken up enthusiastically by quite a few business school academics. It trades on the idea of the liberal arts, the humanities, and suggests that the business school curriculum needs to widen to include more about the practice of management. The 2011 US Carnegie report into management education made much of this, suggesting that the business school needed to connect with other parts of the university, and see its task as including character formation.[7]

There are two parts to this suggestion I think. One is to say that the sort of research and teaching that happens within the business school can be enriched by the inclusion of methodologies and topics not commonly seen to be part of its remit. So this could be an encouragement for qualitative research into what it is like to manage or to be managed, for the use of literary texts or films as teaching aids or resources for research, for the teaching of philosophy and history. This would certainly enlarge the imagination of the business school, and (within the context of the university) provide incentives for its inhabitants to visit other parts of campus.

Behind this, however, is a more radical suggestion: that the purpose of this sort of education is to do with character formation, the shaping of the minds of those who are passing through. Rather than just teaching techniques, the business school should be concerned with Plato's education of the guardians – providing self-knowledge, wisdom, empathy. If the problem is that the current products of the school are pointy heads with ideas above their station, then make them read Emile Zola, study what Emmanuel Levinas says about ethics, and watch films about the tragic consequences of getting rich too quickly. That way, when they graduate, their eyes will have been raised from the spreadsheet, and their imaginations concerning the lives of others will have been enlarged.

MBA: More Bad Advice

A slightly different diagnosis of the problem, though one that starts in a similar place, finds powerful expression in *Managers not MBAs*, by the Canadian business academic, Henry Mintzberg.[8] Starting from the proposition that managing is a practical matter, Mintzberg suggests that if business schools want to help create better leaders, then they need to stop assuming that the classroom is the right place to do it. He echoes the rest in suggesting that the MBA curriculum is too narrow, too focused on finance, and that it tends to ignore leadership and management. When the curriculum does address the problem, the assumption is that such matters can be fed through the theory-machine in order to produce testable hypotheses and teachable procedures. Mintzberg insists that this can never be the case, that management is a skill, an art based on insight, vision and intuition, a form of wisdom that comes from having done many things and having understood the complexity of the world. It's a humanist and pragmatist position, one grounded in the specificities of being in the world with other human beings, combined with a modesty about what can be achieved.

The problem that critics of this kind identify is that most academics have never managed anything apart from their careers, so no wonder they prefer theory to practice, the classroom to the world. It is this isolation, combined with a certain sort of arrogance, that encourages people to believe that it is not necessary to know something about a particular business in order to manage it. (Though if academics are threatened to be managed by someone from outside the groves of academe, this generalization is rapidly set aside and educational experience is demanded.) The sort of leadership which is taught to MBAs also encourages not listening because you think that you already know, a conceit that comes from believing that 'management' means not getting stuck in the dull details, but helicoptering in order to see the big picture. The answer, for Mintzberg and others, is to honour practice, both in terms of a cautiousness about the universal application of management theories, but also to see management education as a practical matter, as something which requires modes of teaching which are more like those you might find in other professional schools such as medicine and architecture. This means learning by doing, and getting out of the classroom to experience what it is like to deal with different situations, and perhaps be able to offer good advice.

Professionalization

Both the liberal arts and the pragmatist responses to the dominance of finance in the business school are essentially aimed at the curriculum, whether making students study Nietzsche or getting them to dig holes in the road. There is another response which is more institutional, in the sense that it is aimed at rethinking the goal of the business school: why not imagine that management is a profession, and treat schooling as professional training? In a general sense, it is easy enough to claim that management is a profession, in the sense that it is largely well-compensated work, mostly indoors, which requires some sort of qualification. But calling something a profession – in the same way that law, medicine and teaching are professions – also has some specific assumptions about licensing by the state, about the codes of practice that they adhere to, and the forms of self-regulation that they employ. At the moment, no one can be barred from being a manager, whatever their transgressions in previous organizations.

In a rather well-known essay from 2008, two business school academics argued that management might not be a profession at the moment, but it should be one.[9] Again invoking the spectre of lost legitimacy (and at the very moment that banks were crashing all around), Rakesh Khurana and Nitin Nohria suggested that 'true' professions have codes of conduct, a governing body which oversees certifications, and some sort of implicit contract with the public. This is an endearingly old-fashioned view of the professions, almost a nostalgic one, but a powerful way of thinking about a new role for the business school. It could become one of the sites for the production of a new profession, a place which combined the teaching of skills and knowledge with the production of a social character who could be admired.

In their article, Khurana and Nohria outline a Hippocratic oath for managers, in which the intending manager has to swear (and I'm abbreviating considerably here) to serve society, balance different interests, act lawfully, honestly and without consideration of personal benefit, treat everyone equally, consult widely and always act to uphold the standards of the profession. Versions of the oath were sworn at Harvard, and some other b-schools, in the wake of the financial crash. They also suggest that some sort of accrediting body administer an exam which all graduating students would have to take before they were licensed as professional managers, and that infractions to the code could result in individuals being struck off, perhaps blighting their careers if they were honest enough to admit that on a job application (which seems unlikely, given that they have hardly displayed noble character traits up to that point).

It's a very stimulating thought experiment though, and one that is mentioned often by those who wish to encourage some change in the business school. Khurana and Nohria do acknowledge some obvious problems – that management doesn't have a formalized body of knowledge, that a 'code' might stifle innovation (supposedly the lifeblood of management), and that there is no particular agreement on the 'function' of management anyway – but the attractions of rethinking the b-school as a professional school are clear. It would provide a clear purpose, a set of comparator schools to measure against, and perhaps make it less embarrassing to explain what you do for a living when talking to the professor of literature. But there is another problem too, which is that many people actually perform 'management' functions, but only a few get paid for doing them. As I have already suggested, management is as much a claim about the importance of a particular occupational group as a description of what they do, and it's a leaky claim, because all of us are engaged in organizing. But more of that in Chapters 6 and 7.

Greedy bastards

The easiest summary of all the above, and one that would inform most people's understandings of what goes on in the b-school, is that they are places that teach people how to get money out of the pockets of ordinary people and keep it for themselves. In some senses, that's a description of capitalism, but there is also a sense here that business schools actually teach, in the reptilian words of Gordon Gekko from the film *Wall Street*, that 'greed is good'. As one US business school dean opined, 'The way business schools today compete leads students to ask, "What can I do to make the most money?" and the manner in which faculty members teach allows students to regard the moral consequences of their actions as mere afterthoughts.'[10] The subject of business is both the educational programme and its product – that is, a person who subjects themselves to their career as a project of the self.

There are a few dimensions to this. One is the idea that the gloomy science of neoliberal economics, to use Ghoshal's phrasing, teaches people that they and others are self-interested. This is a theory of human motivation that assumes that the individual is always looking after their own interests and, if correct, then would encourage us all to behave selfishly because only an idiot is going to be generous in a jungle. To suggest that human beings are tied together by political institutions, ethical codes, moral practices, values, or culture is just the sort of motherhood-and-apple-pie crap that gets in the way of hungry people being successful. One insider study suggests this silence about moral issues is encouraged by the sort of stance taken in the notes for the teaching cases at Harvard Business School, the poster child of b-schools.[11] There seems to be a suggestion that students should be guided by moral considerations, but silence about what these might be – a moral relativism that the author of the study suggests condones pretty much any form of behaviour.

Another element of the verdict of greed is that the greedy just can't wait to push their noses into the trough. This is the idea that selfishness encourages short-term utility maximization, not long-run strategies that rely on predictability and co-operation and build long-term relationships with suppliers, banks, customers and so on. The way that business school marketing and rankings work supports this type of account of human nature, stressing as it does salary levels after graduation, or holding out the possibility of promotion, a nice car and lots of trips in aeroplanes. (Insert here an imaginary picture of someone with a good haircut striding towards the camera, or gesturing in a meeting room while other people look on, admiringly.)

These speculative and moralizing arguments are, to some extent, backed up by research, though some of this is of dubious quality. There are various surveys of business school students which suggest that they have an instrumental approach to education; that is to say, they want what b-school marketing and branding tells them that they want. In terms of the classroom, they expect the teaching of uncomplicated and practical concepts and tools which they believe will be helpful to them in their future careers. Philosophy is for the birds. As someone who has taught in business schools for twenty years, this sort of finding doesn't surprise me, though others suggest rather more incendiary findings. One US survey compared MBA students to people who were imprisoned in low-security prisons and found that the latter were more ethical. Another suggested that the likelihood of committing some form of corporate crime increased if the individual concerned had experience of graduate business education, or military service. (Both careers presumably involve absolving responsibility to an organization.) Other surveys suggest that students come in believing in employee well-being and customer satisfaction and leave thinking that shareholder value is the most important issue, and that business school students are more likely to cheat than students in other subjects.[12]

Whether the causes and effects (or indeed the findings) are as neat as surveys like this might suggest is something that I doubt, but it would be equally daft to suggest that the business school has no effect on its graduates. Having an MBA might not make a student greedy, impatient, unethical, or whatever, but (as I argued in Chapter 2) both its explicit and hidden curriculum does teach lessons. Not that these lessons are acknowledged when something goes wrong, because then the business school usually denies all responsibility. That's a tricky position though because, as a 2009 *Economist* editorial put it 'You cannot claim that your mission is to "educate the leaders who make a difference to the world" and then wash your hands of your alumni when the difference they make is malign.'[13]

After the 2007 crash, there was a game of pass-the-blame-parcel going on, so it's not surprising that most business school deans were also trying to blame consumers for borrowing too much, the bankers for behaving so riskily, rotten apples for being so bad, and the system for being, well, the system. Who, after all, would want to claim that they merely taught greed?

SLOPPY AND IRRELEVANT

Business schools have been blamed for many things, so no wonder that their academics feel abused and misunderstood. In studies of animal behaviour, when a creature is stressed, it can engage in ritualized 'displacement' behaviour – preening, scratching, feeding and so on. This is usually accounted for in terms of a conflict between two drives – for example, wanting to be near something but also being scared of it.

In a marvellous example of displacement activity, a paper war has been going on for some time within the business school world, usually called the 'rigour-relevance' debate.[14] It's really a re-run of the eternal schizophrenia that the business school is continually afflicted with. It wants to be like the university, and be liked by the university, and be accorded the same respect that proper disciplines receive. That's why the b-school has professors and journals and degrees and conferences and all the other paraphernalia of the academy. However, when it does this, it's accused of being too ivory tower, of not being able to impact on the actual practices of flesh-and-blood managers in the real world, out there in the university of life. But if it moves too close to real-world management, leaving campus, getting its hands dirty (or at least, sustaining a few paper-cuts), then the snobbish apparatus of the university condemns it for not being a proper subject at all, just a trade that is allowed on campus if it keeps on bringing in the money.

It's an endless merry-go-round, but each side has its solutions to the problems with the business school. On the 'rigour' side, there are plenty of b-school academics who wish to defend academic practices, usually of the US technocratic business school variety. They are convinced that some version of the scientific method is the sure path to better knowledge about management. On the 'relevance' side are those who wish to argue that for business schools to chase academic brownie points is a distraction from what they should really be doing: educating managers. Various voices bemoan the lack of engagement between the things that interest academic researchers and the things that managers care about. The narrow disciplinary focus of most academics, patrolling their corridors and fields, finding gaps in the literature, means that there is a failure to see the big picture. In most of these Balkanized sub-disciplines, there is also a premium placed on theory development, or rather, on theory that corrects other theory. In terms of teaching, there is a misalignment between the goals of academic programmes and the factors needed for managerial success. The conclusion is that the business school has been captured or hijacked by the university, and that it needs to be rescued, like a princess in an ivory tower.

It seems to me that the rigour/relevance debate is a shadow play of the wider issues that face the b-school. Even though it has been played out on a largely nostalgic and modernizing terrain, either defending some notion of the university in the name of science or attacking it in the name of progress, it speaks to the wider issues of what the business school is for, and who it is for. Rarely is it asked who the rigour or relevance is aimed at, largely because it is assumed that this means managers in large capitalist organizations. As a displacement activity, the 'debate' is entertaining to watch, but as a way of thinking about the wider problems with the b-school, it almost entirely misses the point. But then perhaps that is the point, because if the participants asked more pointed questions, things might start getting uncomfortable. And no one wants that.

DON'T ROCK THE BOAT

I started off by suggesting that it was remarkable that so much of the criticism of the b-school comes from within, rather than without. I also noted that it was remarkable that the apparatus of the school simply digests such criticisms without a rumble or a fart, even submitting their published versions for ranking exercises, and promoting the people who successfully air their opinions in highly regarded journals. It's a measure of the futility of all that sound and fury, and perhaps also tells us something about the nature of the criticisms being voiced.

In general, these are complaints that rapidly get embedded in detail, by paper debates in which Professor A corrects Professor B on their interpretation of whatever it was that Professor C said, many years ago. That is what academics do, of course, inheriting a scholastic tradition which worries about the substance of angels, and rewards those who write their worries down. Even those who claim to be concerned with the suffering of others, and aim their theory at the powerful in the name of making a new world, are rarely very specific about what they would actually change, if they were leader of the republic for a day. This is what one commentator suggests involves

> ... recommending little, prescribing naught ... expressed as a kind of vigilance ... These radicals of the impasse celebrate the virtues of intellectual caution and scholarly calculation that have, we cannot help but notice, the convenient effect of justifying their continued employment.[15]

Academic debates are slow, careful, nit-picking, and to some extent that is a value to be prized. But don't be distracted by the style of the debate, because there is another much more important issue here too.

If you asked monks to critically assess monasteries, curators to have a really good think about museums, or doctors to consider hospitals, they would say lots of things which were of interest but are most unlikely to demand radical changes in the structure of an institution that puts bread on their tables. Their complaints are likely to be internal, in the sense of re-arranging certain matters, altering this and tweaking that. Now these might be worthwhile tweaks, but they are unlikely to be radical, in the sense of really thinking about the purpose of the institution. Rather, they would assume that it was a good thing, and proceed from there. And so it is with most of the critics I have surveyed in this chapter.

Let me summarize what they end up saying. They propose being more like a proper university department, or less like a traditional university department, or more like a professional school, or closer links with the arts and humanities, or closer links with business. We are told that there is too much finance and neoclassical economics and that there should be more of something else. They suggest changing the structure of rankings of teaching or research, changing the b-school's marketing and branding strategies, or reforming its governance structures and organizational culture.[16] They propose that deans should behave differently, and that everyone needs to understand the grand challenges that are facing the world. New courses and themes are put forward, on ethics, corporate social responsibility, the environment, on businesses in society. There are many well-meaning injunctions about teaching in different ways, aimed at changing the subjectivities and group dynamics of students or soliciting ethical leadership.[17] We are told that business schools need to recapture a sense of moral authority, of legitimacy, and that this might involve remembering an older version of the business school, or inventing a new one. No one suggests calling the bulldozers in.

Many of the changes being proposed (though not all I think) are good and sensible ones, and would produce a better, kinder version of the business school. But very few of the critics really address the central issue – that this is a factory for producing employees for capitalist organizations, a machine for producing a very particular kind of future. Instead there is a recitation going on here, an incantation of words such as 'ethics', 'morality' and 'responsibility'. Combine those with words like 'reinvention', 'transformation', 'rethinking' and you have a powerful set of spells to keep the dark away, and make it seem that the critics are doing their work. Consciences can be salved without the danger of losing a job or a decent pension, and the changes being proposed are vague enough that they can be repeated insistently, because we always need more ethics and morality. (How could we ever have enough?) And nothing ever seems to change, so the critics are justified in repeating their complaints, and getting them published in well-regarded journals in which they lucidly explain what is going wrong, but avoid suggesting what should be done. And anyway, the thing keeps growing whatever they say, because the students keep coming. Despite all the noise in the critical corner, the b-school seems to work well for all those

who are parts of it – academics, students, university administrators, taxpayers, publishers and the makers of gowns. And the
vice-chancellors? Well, they might not like the b-school's brash
vulgarity either, but they need its money.

The next chapter completes my survey of the current state
we are in by saying something about the institution that houses
lots of business schools: the university itself. Many of the critics
propose turning (back) to the university, but is the university also
becoming a business school?

5

The business school and the university

The 1959 report which called for the professionalization of the US business school and inaugurated its technocratic manifestation perceptively suggested that the b-school was

> ... an uncertain giant, gnawed by doubt and harassed by the barbs of unfriendly critics. It seeks to serve several masters and is assured by its critics that it serves none well. The business world takes its students but deprecates the value of their training, extolling instead the virtues of science and the liberal arts. It finds itself at the foot of the academic table uncomfortably nudging those other two stepchildren, Education and Agriculture.[1]

The problem of the business school is inextricably entangled with the problem of the university and its relation to the world, and this is an old problem. In his 1776 *The Wealth of Nations*, Adam Smith complains about the lack of teaching, the Latin and Greek, the refusal to change and the poor preparation for life which the universities of the time provided. Famously, he complained that they were a 'sanctuary in which exploded systems and obsolete prejudices find shelter and protection after they have been hunted out of every corner of the world'. Immanuel Kant, in his 1798 essay *The Conflict of the Faculties*, considers the difficult relations between the lower (philosophical) faculties of the university and the higher (worldly) ones, concluding that the autonomy of the lower was needed to ensure that the latter could help achieve the goal of human freedom. But he assumed that there would always be a tension between them, and that thinking and the demands of the world could never ultimately be reconciled. Rather more definitively, Cardinal Henry Newman, in the 1852 *The Idea of a University*, insisted that professional education had no place at all in his idea of the university:

> ... without directly qualifying a man for any of the employments of life, it enriches and ennobles all. Without teaching him the particular business of any one office or calling, it enables him to act his part in each of them with better grace and more elevated carriage.

Thorstein Veblen echoes this hostility to the utilitarians in his 1918 *Higher Learning in America*, an attack on the bureaucratization and professionalization of the university. He refers to the corporate university, run by the 'captains of erudition' as an 'abomination of desolation'. Let's just say that the academy has not been welcoming towards people who do things in the world, unless they just bring their money and then leave.

Not all business schools are part of a university; indeed, in some countries they tend to be free-standing institutions, but most business schools claim the status that being a 'higher' education institution confers. If they were merely schools, or training colleges, or purveyors of certificates in this and that advertising in the back of trade magazines, or even shouting their wares from the back of a truck, they would have a much harder time moving the product. The idea of the university is one that gives certain forms of knowledge a sprinkling of medieval fairy dust, a patina of legitimacy that has taken centuries to adhere. Of course, this is a legitimacy that reflects power, most particularly the place of the university as a finishing school for the male children of the elites. As we saw in Chapter 1, it begins as a feudal history, and then becomes a capitalist one, always inscribed with exclusions of gender, religion, ethnicity and so on. Despite (or perhaps because of) all that gentleman's club selection and the pomposity that went with it, the *universitas* of 1088 is an institution that is now global.[2] The resonance of the idea of the university therefore makes it much easier to brand the 'U of Wherever' with caps and gowns and Latin and Greek, and for its b-school to combine a greybeard's solemn dignity with a passionate boosterism about our collective futures.

In many countries across the world, but particularly the UK, universities are gradually moving into the private sector. The proportion of money provided by the state is declining year by year, and is being substituted for by tuition fees and various business activities. As well as making money selling to students their accommodation, food and entertainment, universities are moving into conference organization, fully funded research, training and consultancy, commercial publishing, licensing of their brand, private sponsoring of chairs and buildings, spin-off companies and so on. The advance guard of this new understanding of academic capitalism are the business schools. They can sell their courses for the highest premiums, with even low-ranked institutions being able to command improbable sums of money for an English-language postgraduate degree

Following on from the previous chapter, if we want to deal with the many problems posed by the business school, then we also need to think about what university education is for. If it is assumed that a university must simply compete with other providers to sell customers the certificates that they are told that they need, then intervention in such a market would be unlikely to have any purchase. But this is not actually what universities do. A whole host of regulatory authorities and legal statutes – professional groups, employers' associations, accreditation bodies, health and safety laws, national benchmarks – already shape the contents of higher education in very significant ways. There is no reason to assume that business and management education cannot, or should not, also be subject to similar forms of regulation, rather than being a commodity which is shaped by the ideology and practice of the market. If someone studies to become a dentist, we would not assume that the curriculum was designed around what students thought should be included on a programme in dentistry. So, why assume this of business and management?

In their introduction to a special issue of the elite US journal *Academy of Management Learning and Education*, two distinguished UK business school academics muse on the legitimacy and impact of their employers.[3] It's an odd piece, with some preliminary throat clearing on how we might define 'legitimacy' and 'impact', combined with an awful lot of claims that 'more research is needed.' That is what academics tend to do, I suppose: worry a lot about definitions and then try to get someone else to pay for them to worry some more. It's nice work, if you can get it. As I keep saying, I should know because I am one of them. But what struck me as strange about this discussion of legitimacy was just how a-political it was. As if the question of what the business school is and does could be discussed in calm voices by sensible people in a nice room with a buffet delivered at lunchtime. And the people invited into that room would be business leaders, deans of business schools, MBA students and alumni, and state policy makers. These, it seems, are the 'stakeholders' that matter, and they need to be provided with well-funded research findings by business school academics in order to make their decisions wisely.

See any problems with that picture? It's pretty much of a piece with what I have been arguing is the deeply entrenched myopia in b-school logic, that it claims some sort of (social) scientific legitimacy – the privilege of the university – but effectively only engages in a conversation with the people who pay the bills. Fair enough, you might say, because any business needs to satisfy its customers. If it didn't do that, it would disappear, and all the business schools would be boarded up and become homes for nesting birds and scuttling rats.

The problem here is that the people who pay the bills are by no means the only ones who are affected by what goes on in business schools, or who might have questions about the legitimacy of the forms of knowledge that are sold by those institutions. The US home owners with foreclosed properties based on sub-prime mortgages in 2008, the 1,129 people who died in the 2013 Rana Plaza sweatshop building collapse in Bangladesh, the boarded-up shops on the high streets of the city I come from in Northern England, the 100,000 people who live in Kiribati in the Southern Pacific and will see their island disappear in half a century – all these are impacted by the sort of knowledge being sold by business schools. All of these, and many many more, are stakeholders in what the business school teaches and researches.

This might seem hyperbolic, but again consider the reverse. Would business school academics want to argue that what they did only had an impact on other academics? Would they want to claim that the business school had no effect on its students, on managers in companies, on state policy makers and so on? That the business school was just an echo chamber, a gaggle of pointy-heads mumbling at each other and having a nap in the afternoon? It might be fun to say it, but it's very unlikely to be the case, and there are plenty of examples of concepts and practices that have spread from the business school to business – from 'relationship marketing' and 'corporate culture' to the Black-Scholes model of financial derivatives. As we have seen, business schools like to loudly claim that what they do makes a difference and then to use that claim to sell the products that they offer.

So if the 'stakeholders' for the business school are widely spread and multiple, and if it is an institution which is responsible for producing the machineries of the future, then shouldn't we insist that (as Spiderman has so wisely taught us) with great power comes great responsibility? More of that later in the book, but first, let's look at some of the ways in which the business school has influenced the practice of the university itself. What are universities for?

THE PARASITE AND THE HOST

Universities are normally places that we might imagine to be generous exporters of knowledge. They might have begun by being modelled as cloisters, walled against outsiders, but their reputation rests on their ability to scatter ideas into the world. It doesn't matter for my purposes whether these ideas involve theories about the beginning of the universe, histories of the papacy, or cures for cancer. Academics labour over ideas and then send those ideas into the world by teaching them to students, writing them down in books and journals, or producing techniques or products that can be spun out into new companies. This knowledge is made within but used without. It is incubated, polished and then disseminated.

The business school is a little different though. As we have already seen, it clearly does produce knowledge to be sent out into the world, but its knowledges are also increasingly being used to restructure the university itself. This usually isn't a direct process, in the sense of academics from within a particular university advising their employers on that university's strategy, or the details of particular accounting methods. Indeed, most university managers appear not to enthusiastically welcome advice from their employees on how to run the institution, even if they are academics who specialize in business, and whose expertise is lauded in the marketing of the business school.[4] Rather than a direct flow of ideas then, the policy and financial environment which shapes the university, and which has been partly shaped by the business school, is increasingly reflecting back business school assumptions. This is because they have percolated into funding bodies, research agencies, producers of ranking lists, careers advisors, publishers, providers of research data and so on. The dominant assumption is that the student is a customer who chooses a product, and the university a business that provides it.

This is an unusual state of affairs. Despite long-standing expertise in geography, physics, medicine and so on, none of those disciplines have come to reshape the university in fundamental ways – unless we count the production of maps of campus, electric light in buildings and longer-lived employees. Indeed, it might be said that the business school is the cuckoo in the nest, gradually reshaping the university, redefining academic function and purpose. This is knowledge which is being produced *by* the university which is gradually *changing* the university, a sort of hormone produced within the corporate body that alters how that body works. No wonder that so many academics from other parts of the university treat the business school with suspicion. Its project appears to be an imperial one, making the speculations of cosmologists and the hermeneutics of literary critics seem grounded and modest by comparison. The university is becoming a business school.

SELLING ENGLAND BY THE POUND

Much as I enjoy blaming them, this isn't just a question of university presidents, vice chancellors or rectors being seduced by management gurus and special government advisors talking of excellence, productivity and quality. University bosses have certainly embraced their new 'chief executive' status, particularly the pay and perks that go with it, but they are not responsible for the political and economic environment which shapes and constrains their decision making. If we take the UK as an example, over the past two decades, universities have effectively been privatized without the general public really noticing. It wasn't done by selling shares, but by gradually withdrawing public funding and replacing it with student loans and loud imprecations to institutions to become more entrepreneurial. As an example, take the place where I work at the time of writing – the University of Leicester. Despite it being in some sense a public corporation, only about a quarter of its income in 2015–16 came from the state, and most of that was in the areas of science, technology and medicine. In all UK universities, teaching in the social sciences and humanities now effectively receives no state subsidy at all. The business school is one of those areas.

What has differentiated the UK business school from other parts of the social sciences and humanities has been its capacity to earn large amounts of money for its host university. Initially this was largely through the MBA, and then as that began to decline it was replaced by masters programmes in various management specialisms (marketing, accounting and so on) and largely aimed at non-EU students. Since the tripling of undergraduate fees in 2012, to £9,000 per year, the increased fee income from undergraduates has also become significant, particularly since business and management is the largest undergraduate subject across UK universities. It is not an overstatement to say that the expansion of business school income is what has allowed successive UK governments to move to partial privatization of the entire sector. Around one in seven students are now studying business or a related topic and without that revenue stream, reductions in the state-provided block grant would have been catastrophic and probably politically impossible. The business school prevented the marketizing university from collapsing into bankruptcy. It made the politically impossible possible.

Business school income was an enabler in other senses too. As UK universities become hooked on the money coming in, so did they begin to see students as customers who might take their money elsewhere. I suppose in some sense they always had been, but the ties between student choices and university finances were becoming much more tightly connected, because they were no longer mediated by the distribution of collected taxes by the welfare state and a state university grants committee. Relaxations to the constraints on numbers of students that were previously centrally allocated to universities and courses meant that student numbers could potentially be much more variable. This was now a market, with students as purchasers and other universities as competitors. Courses and departments became income streams, and calculations of their relative 'surplus' or 'contribution' became standard tools for the management of the university. Departments that failed to meet their contribution targets were berated, starved of resources and possibly merged or closed. University finance meetings became a jungle, red in tooth and claw, with the extinction of subjects that didn't pay their way being a very real possibility.

It follows from this that in order to move your department or university from the bottom right quadrant into the top left, more income needs to be made while less is spent on other inputs. 'Doing more with less', 'working smarter not harder' and other euphemisms simply directed attention away from the fact that lecture sizes were getting bigger, and expensive small group teaching took place less frequently. Higher education in the UK was becoming mass, rationalized, Fordist, McDonaldized, because that was the only way to pay the bills as the state withdrew from funding.[5] The tools of the contemporary business school began to find a place within meetings, organizational structures, marketing plans, mission statements and so on. The language of corporate communication, of bright-eyed claims to be passionate about people and things, became the new normal. The signage was renewed and campus flapped with banners claiming that everyone is number one. Dream jobs are mentioned, and CVs boosted. This and that is claimed to be 'world-class', or 'world-beating'. Quotes from a diverse range of happy students are solicited, and the more attractive ones get their photos taken.

Strategies must be conjured, customers must be found, and products need to be sold. This meant spending more money – on marketing and advertising, on signature campus redevelopments to show off to visitors on open days, on relentless product innovation to give the customer what they want, on accreditations, and on strategies to claw up league tables by engaging in positional games.

It's an irony that once universities begin competing with each other for students, because income from taxpayers is going down, they begin to face a lot of costs that they weren't incurring before. Markets, it appears, are not that efficient after all. The number of people employed by the university in doing marketing, strategy, quality, leadership and so on increases. Markets are expensive things to play, and if you don't have any particular reputational advantages – as Oxford and Cambridge do, for example – then you need to keep spending just to stay in the game. And this includes spending on 'excellent' leaders too, because they need highly competitive reward packages commensurate with their responsibilities. And so the wheel starts to spin, and more money needs to be spent to make more money. The logic of the market, the logic of the business school, embeds itself into the interstices of the university and burrows in so deep that it becomes part of the place. More resources get sucked from teaching into central university functions which in turn need to be paid for by raising income, which in turn requires more marketing and so on. It's a nice case study of the costs of markets, and one that directly contradicts the simple truism that – all things being equal – markets drive costs down and quality up.

And finally, the 'business-fication' of the university changes academics too. They are ranked, and increasingly, they are also branded, as being elements in what the university sells. On the website, professors smile woodenly in well-lit photographs, text dripping with inflated claims to importance. Brand ambassadors in good clothes. Within the b-school, and increasingly in other disciplines too, the ranking of academic journals means that only certain kinds of publications count, and one person's publications become directly comparable to the person in the office next door. The anxiety that this generates encourages the sort of behaviour which allows the business university to be run with maximum efficiency. When people are made comparable as numbers for management purposes, it encourages those people to compare themselves to each other as well. Ranking and branding are managerial technologies that frame employees' expectations of success and failure. Should I publish here? Should I say this? What grading will the students give me? How many citations do I have? The usefulness of rankings is confirmed by the stabilization of the sort of behaviour which rankings produces. This means that the movements within rankings are relatively minor, and the congealing of a hierarchy both produces and is produced by academics who are engaged in positional strategies too. The corporatization of the university tends towards a social and intellectual closure, a narrowing of practices and expectations amongst academics who are driven by the need to do whatever is necessary to get into, or stay in, an institution with an elevated position in the rankings.[6]

All that being said, the UK is an extreme case, because in a period of twenty years it has moved from being an elite higher education (HE) system that was almost entirely state funded to a mass higher education system that the state largely regulates, as well as underwriting an increasingly gigantic amount of student debt. This is not a change that is mirrored in other nation states, each having a different balance between state and student funding. Indeed, in large parts of north-western Europe, the state is still heavily invested in supporting universities on the grounds that they are part of the public sector, a set of institutions which (like nurseries, schools and colleges) produce the citizens who will be the teachers, doctors and artists of tomorrow. In that sense, I need to be careful not to overgeneralize the UK case. However, what does seem to be true is that in all national HE systems the university sector is gradually becoming closer to the market rather than the state. The direction of travel is towards some sort of pricing (however it is described), more commercial activities, the establishment of private universities and so on. It also means more teaching in English, in order to attract high fee-paying foreign students, which in turn presses towards teaching concepts and theories which originate from English-speaking countries. The market in students, as it becomes global, is a market which appears to encourage the use of a global language, global ranking systems, and standardized qualifications. In search of legibility and competitive advantage, real distinctiveness and local specificity are discouraged. Instead, a simulacrum of difference is presented, one in which the website advertises a global product but decorates it with local colour.

THE IDEAS OF THE BUSINESS SCHOOL

The irony of the victory of the business school is that it might end up as the death of the university. The parasite transforms its host, or kills it. The techniques and language required for this transformation of the university into something else were already there in the shiny atrium of the business school. (A place that, intellectually, most other people in the university were actually rather sceptical about, and probably still are.) The business school teaches that employees can be motivated, that customers can be persuaded to spend money, that leadership can be transformative, that business is international, that technology brings market advantages, that markets produce efficient outcomes and so on. B-school knowledge provides a template for how the university can become a global knowledge corporation like any other. The business school dissolves local difference, makes money and ideas commensurable and mobile. It is both a loudspeaker and an exemplar of the idea that anything has a price, and that what is sold should be shaped in ways that make it sellable. Knowledge that appears to have no population of customers willing to pay for it will simply not be produced, just as useless products will end up in discount shops or landfill sites.

In that sense, in some parts of the world, the business school has won. It has colonized the university and its logic is now found everywhere, on all of its corridors. Let's hear it for the business school, the saviour of the university. A bigger loss lurks though, because the only thing that distinguished the university from the training college or consultancy company was the idea of the university as a distinctive place, somewhere in which knowledge was produced generously, somewhere with loose connections to the urgencies and imperatives of the world. The problem that the university now faces, with its massive and continuing costs of selling its distinctiveness in a crowded marketplace, is how to actually be distinctive. Because if it is a commercial organization like any other, then it will have its various functions outcompeted on price, efficiency, mode of delivery and so on. Other organizations can be more responsive at delivering research results, or teaching at any time of the day or night across 24 different time zones, or returning marked coursework on time, or simply making more money with less staff.

For the last quarter of a century, a variety of authors, usually from the humanities and often from the US, have been bemoaning the death of the university in apocalyptic terms. The university is now in ruins, they say, a zombie institution which has lost its reason to exist. It is animated largely by the interests of capitalist corporations, and can now only be understood in terms of the relation between producers and consumers.[7] As with the b-school critics we met in Chapter 4, these critics are almost always occupying good jobs in good universities, so it seems that their criticisms aren't particularly dangerous, even if they might be accurate. However, what they almost always miss is the importance of the b-school in these changes, and this is usually because they inhabit different buildings, and regard the place as a symptom, not a cause.

The beady eyes of the business school stare out through the face of the university. In its relentless selling of credentials, and its embrace of market mechanisms and management hierarchies, the boundaries between the school of business and everything else are becoming increasingly indistinct. Everything is for sale. Roll up, roll up. In the second half of the book, I will explore the idea that changing the b-school into something else might also help rebuild the university, as well as doing something to reshape our collective futures. To begin that process though, we need to begin by taking management apart. Just what is 'management'?

6

What is 'management' anyway?

In the first half of this book I was trying to convince you that we have a problem. I wanted you to understand that the business school is a place that has a malign influence, and that this is because it acts as the loudspeaker for one particular form of life: market managerial capitalism. It is clear that this is an economic model which is complicit with all sorts of social, economic and environmental problems and that the business school is one of the places that will need to change if we are to collectively deal with the world we have made. More of that in the next chapter, but first I need to pin down the idea of 'management', because this is the practice that is taught within the b-school. (It is also the name for lots of business schools, a name that inserts a certain honesty into its branding as a school that teaches the bosses, not the workers.[1]) This is important because otherwise the slippery word will slide back in, claiming that it is a mutable term that can easily cope with the extensions and modifications that I will be proposing later on.

In this chapter, I will show that it can't, or rather, that we shouldn't let it, slip back in, because the word 'management' already comes with some quite specific baggage. It is a word that arrives with particular meanings, like most words do, and those meanings need to be clearly understood in order that 'management' can be distinguished from all the other social arrangements, patterns and institutions that we find in the ramified and dizzying world of human beings. Bear in mind that this book is arguing that the business school doesn't take the problem of organization seriously enough, and that is what needs to be addressed. In a blindingly obvious sense then, the key to the problem that the business school presents is in the name. Words like 'business', or 'management', or 'commerce' almost always refer us to some very particular forms of organization. Mostly large, mostly private sector, often corporations and almost always supposedly populated by people with no more politics or ethics than Pavlov's dogs. (I pay you, you bark. I praise you, you roll over and show me your belly.)

The business school teaches capitalism and the inevitability of the corporate form. These quite specific organizational models and their paper cut-out rational egoists are then assumed to provide general lessons for all sorts of other organizations, which is a bit like assuming that studying ivy can tell us about all other plants, or that the documented behaviour of elephants must be the same as that of fleas because they are both animals. The fact is that the world of human beings is populated by all sorts of organizations, and they all present different problems of governance, financing and co-ordination. If management is to become a subject worthy of the name, then it must study and teach more than just management. We wouldn't trust a medical school that only studied certain diseases, or restricted its research to people who had a certain skin colour, or that avoided searching for a cure for AIDS because of some moral or political objection to promiscuity or homosexuality. We wouldn't be impressed if a teacher of architecture ignored all buildings that weren't churches, or if a biologist decided to ignore all life forms apart from elephants. This is what the business school is doing with organizations. It is judging all other organizational forms as archaic failures or irrelevant distractions, and assuming that market managerialism is the only and one best way.

But more of this later. First, what is 'management'?

MANAGERY

In English, the word 'management' has an interesting history, and some rather productive differences of meaning. It seems to be derived from the Italian *mano*, hand, and its expansion into *maneggiarre*, the activity of handling and training a horse carried out in a *maneggio* – a riding school. From this form of manual control, the word has expanded into a general activity of training and handling people too.[2] It is a word that originates with ideas of control, of a docile or wilful creature that must be subordinated to the instructions of the master. The later development of the word is also claimed to be influenced by the French *manier* (to handle), *mener* (to lead) and its development into *ménage* – household, or housekeeping – and the verb *ménager* – to economize.

It's a really interesting word, and what the dating of the etymology shows us is that it grows in influence and application as the feudal order of fixed social relations based on ownership of land is disturbed by the rise of a mercantile class. This bourgeois revolution rested upon a relationship to capital, of which land was only one element, but it also relied on more complex forms of production and distribution, and consequently on organizations with more elaborated divisions of labour. Localized craft economies were displaced by manufactories, machine production, urbanization and longer distribution networks via canals and trains. The word is knitted together in the 'dark satanic mills' that romantics and radicals were keen to condemn for the brute people and despoiled landscapes that they produced. But the later imperialism of this word originally designated for handling beasts also follows from its subsequent division into three related meanings – a verb, a noun, and an academic discipline taught in the new *Schola Commercia*.

Management I

First then, the word can be used as a verb. (The same applies with a word like organization, of course, but without any necessary connotations of who or what is doing the organizing. More of that later.) This was originally a verb that can be applied to the need to deal with complex or adverse matters, and it is the oldest way in which the horse-handling word was used in English. In *Richard II* of 1595, Shakespeare has Green tell us 'Now for the rebels which stand out in Ireland, Expedient manage must be made, my liege.' The word could mean something like careful planning, necessary in this case because of the complexity and danger of that which was being faced. The *London Encyclopaedia* of 1829 has an entry for 'Manage' which suggests that it is 'an obsolete synonyme of management, which signifies, guidance; administration; and particularly able or prudent administration of affairs: managery is another (deservedly obsolete) synonyme of this signification: manageable is tractable; easy to be managed.'[3] This sense of management as coping, as dealing with a particular state of affairs is still passable in everyday English. You might ask 'how are you managing?', if someone has told you about some problem that they face, though the word has to a large extent been augmented by an understanding that this is something which is specifically done by people called 'managers' within a formal organization.

When used in this latter way, it implies a separation between the actual doing of whatever is being managed and the higher-level function of controlling these processes. In other words, management as a practice is not intricately involved with any particular form of labour or state of affairs, but is a claim to co-ordinate the doing of all things. As we saw in Chapter 4, what is taught in the business school is not detail, but the grand plan, because you don't need to know about widgets in order to manage them. During the twentieth century, management has become understood as a form of human activity which requires an elevation from the mundane in order to gain a better overall perspective. Though management may be etymologically linked with the hand, it is no longer a practice which is 'hands on' or a word used to describe the element of 'managery' necessary to all human endeavours. Instead, it is a practice which is firmly attached to a particular occupation, a claim of specialist mastery which implicitly denies that others have that capacity, and is justified with reference to embossed certificates from business schools. The idea of an everyday activity of practical coping – one potentially possessed by all humans – has been relabelled, colonized as a talent or skill exclusive to some and not others.

Management II

The second sense of management is as a plural noun for 'manager': the management, the people up there watching us down here. This meaning is found in English from the early eighteenth century, initially with respect to the people who ran a theatre. (And here it is worth remembering that theatres and circuses were closely related, with tractable horses very often used in the latter, as we can see remembered in the name 'Hippodrome'.) From the nineteenth century onwards, the word begins to be used with greater frequency, referring to an occupational group who have engaged in a very successful strategy of collective social mobility over two centuries. From a disparate collection of job-related nouns – owner, supervisor, superintendent, administrator, overman, foreman, clerk – one word now represents anyone engaged in the co-ordination of people and things. Nowadays, we find managers everywhere – in hospitals, universities, trains – and they are deemed to be universally essential. In 2013, it was claimed that 5 million members of the UK workforce had the title 'manager', and that this was a tenfold increase over a century.[4]

Perhaps the most important element here is the idea that managers are always necessary in organizations. In that sense, all management ideas are subordinate to this general assumption which, once accepted, leaves merely the details of what these managers will do because their necessity is assumed. This is the most important part of the b-school's hidden curriculum, an implicit claim that is almost never made but that underpins all that it does. Once assumed to be necessary in all organizations, and to be a status which is desired, the number of people engaged in management increases, as does the number of people called managers, as the term becomes attached to a wider and wider range of jobs. A new class of people has been created, perhaps not in the classical Marxist sense, though that might not be too wide of the mark, but certainly a class in the sense of a concept which pulls together a diverse set of practices and people under one umbrella and claims that they are all doing the same sort of things.

Management III

Finally, 'Management' is often the name of university departments that signifies (paid) engagement in the discipline of reading, writing and talking about what managers do and what management is. It's how I earn a living, and it's what this book is about. This is certainly not a practice that can be separated from the other two senses of management, simply because much of the output of this 'discipline' is shaped by and in turn shapes contemporary practices in both of the other areas. As we have seen, schools of management and business have become a ubiquitous part of higher education across the globe over the last fifty years or so. From its origins in France two centuries ago, and rapid expansion in the US a century ago, elements of commerce, economics, psychology and sociology have congealed into the b-school, the cash-cow for cash-strapped university managers.

Nowadays, Management claims to be a coherent discipline in itself, and (as we have seen) its schools employ specialists to teach and research in human resource management, accounting and finance, marketing, strategy, operations and production management, business ethics and information systems, as well as a dully predictable variety of specialist topics.

And, in case it needed saying again, the vast majority of the output from this global network of hundreds of thousands of texts, professors, schools, ranking agencies, journal publishers, PhDs and conferences is largely supportive of the growth of all three of these meanings of management. It solicits more management as the solution to the problems of the world, including those of the very universities that house their business schools, and that means more managers, which in turn requires more business school academics to teach the knowledge that they need. It's a win, win, win. This is a bubble which has expanded with extraordinary speed, a bubble which has already hardened into the carapace of common sense, solidified by the addition of large amounts of cash.

This isn't to say that there is no criticism of this process, as we saw in Chapters 3 and 4, but it largely bounces off, or is so modest, vague, or obscure in its proposals as to have no effect. Even when a bit more pointed, it is usually published somewhere with a readership which is so tiny and inbred that it makes shouting on the street a better mode of dissemination. Perhaps most sadly from my point of view, Critical Management Studies, the professional goon squad from within the b-school, has made almost no meaningful proposals for large-scale changes to the way that management education operates. Its arguments have tended to stop with a diagnosis of the implications of a particular form of management – culture, total quality, new public, consultancy, or whatever – then sloshed over some contemporary social theory to make the dish taste better. Or there have been injunctions about what should be done in classrooms, in terms of student-centred or problem-based learning, or a decentring of the lecturer, or the introduction of more controversial topics. Often enough this means that the conclusions have gestured towards a better form of management, one that doesn't commit whatever sin has been diagnosed by the person doing the criticism, but that rarely questions the absolute necessity of management itself, or suggests alternative forms of organization which do not assume permanent hierarchies.[5] This ends up being a form of criticism which avoids criticizing its most obvious target, as if a communist refused to say anything about alternatives to capitalism, or a feminist was silent on what a different gender order should look like.

WHAT DO MANAGERS DO?

The anarchist art critic Herbert Read, in an essay published during the Second World War, entitled 'The Cult of Leadership', suggested that there was a close link between a conception of leadership and a fascist politics. Warming to his theme, he suggests that the opposition to leadership is 'collective responsibility', in which members of the 'body politic' are differentiated according to their function, but socially equal. Even those 'whose function is to co-ordinate others' are just one part of that functioning whole, no more or less important than all the other parts:

> These are the organizers, the administrators and the managers who are essential to a complicated industrial society; but I see no reason why the co-ordinator should be more highly placed or more highly paid than the originator, the creator, the worker. The manager owes his present status and prestige, not to the nature of his work, but to his immediate control of the instruments of production. In any natural society he would be as unobtrusive as a railway signal-man in his box.[6]

It's a nice image, the idea of the quiet, almost invisible co-ordinator, perhaps tipping his hat as you go by. A modest Fat Controller.[7] Someone whose job is to help other people get on with theirs. The opposition that Read is seeking here is with the power-mad dictator, someone who needs a cult to worship them and a chorus to sing them to their bed.

Seventy years after Read was writing, we have been collectively persuaded that you need to be an expert to organize, and that the signal-man is more important than the driver, or indeed anyone else. That's why managers, leaders, executives are now paid such outrageous sums, because they are now imagined to be the most important part of any organization. Selling this idea has been a well-paid job too. The experts have texts, courses, or consultancy to take to market, but in order to make money, they have to construct the idea of a certain lack in the target market. If you want to get someone to buy something, you need to persuade them that they need it, and that you have it. Hence, when it comes to matters of management, it is assumed that we need someone who has management expertise to help us do it, because management must be done, and we can't do it ourselves.

Distilling the practice, occupation and form of knowledge down a bit then, what are the key elements of management as a form of organizing? First, the idea that there is a distinct set of activities which can be called 'management', and that these are different from the sort of things that ordinary people do in coping with most of their lives, when dealing with the troubles and anxieties that the world throws at them. This is a slightly puzzling claim, because many of the things that are done as part of management are just the same as the things that all human beings do – talking, paying attention to things, making sense of things, counting things, writing things down. Unlike someone who makes shoes, plays a musical instrument, or replaces corneas in an eye operation, there doesn't seem to be anything that particular about the things that are involved in doing management such that it would be possible to say to someone else 'Look, I'm doing management now', 'This is what management looks like.' So the claim must be that it is not the practices themselves but the ways that they are done which make them particularly special. To do management must mean that you talk in a particular way, count certain things using specific methods, or make sense of the organization in a way that other people cannot.

It's a claim, in other words, but a slightly odd one. It relies a lot on the persuasive powers of the person or institution making it because it's difficult to see how it could be 'seen' in any other way. And that brings us onto the second part of this, which is that the claim is made by, or on behalf of, managers. Almost all claims about the distinctiveness of the practice of managing are given substance because they are descriptions of something that a manager is doing. So if a manager is talking, they are doing management, whilst if a worker is talking, they aren't. If a manager writes some things down, they are producing a strategy document, whilst if a worker does that, they are keeping records. To investigate what management is, we apparently need to look at what managers do, or say that they do – a tautological definition, and one that contains no reference to practices which are any different to things that a reasonably competent human adult can do. If a shoemaker said that he does what shoemakers do, we could agree to watch him, and see the way that he holds the hammer and the nails, bends the leather over the last, cuts the sole and so on. But if we watched a manager, we would see nothing unusual, nothing that we could not do ourselves. It would be a dull few hours, and there would be no pair of shoes at the end of it (unless they were managing somebody else who was making the shoes of course).

However, one of the things that managers, and their cheerleaders in the b-school, do claim that is unique concerns their ubiquity. There are no other occupations which we would find in almost every industry and sector of the economy, regardless of the organization's size, age, market and so on. Managers appear to be needed everywhere, which makes me wonder just how anything at all happened before they were invented, conjured into being in the steaming vats of the *Schola Commercia*. It might well be that it is the emptiness of any definition of management as a practice that allows them to, chameleon-like, insert themselves anywhere. Since they have no specific expertise, such as in bending leather or using scalpels, they can move between organizations in a way that someone with defined training, experience, or qualifications would not be able. In other contexts, someone might describe this as a confidence trick, the ability to present yourself as an expert in order to extract money from other people. If so, it is a collective trick of huge proportions, and one greatly aided by the fact that the marks who are doing the hiring really do seem to believe that they need the skills that managers claim to offer. (But then they are managers themselves, so doubtless recognize good management when they see it.)

One might think that these levels of ambiguity would mean that the aspiring manager had a difficult position in the labour market, unlike workers with clearly defined skills. However, this is clearly not the case, and the nature of a manager's engagement with an employer is quite specific, it always being assumed that they should occupy the most elevated positions within the organization or their department within it. It is effectively a requirement for an organization with a cadre of managers that it have a clearly defined hierarchy of power and authority in order that they have somewhere to perch so that they can look down. And, as if it weren't enough to have that particular structural position, management also requires that the office holder be paid more than most other people in the organization, as well as having certain perks, such as separate toilets, a personal parking space and a secretary for the dull stuff.

Finally, of course, the claim to be an expert with no specific expertise, and to expect the delicious combination of authority and high pay, is greatly supported if some sort of external body can provide a qualification which makes those claims on behalf of the bearer. It's the MBA certificate and its derivatives that fills in the gap, for an occupation that would otherwise have no allies to buttress its privileges. Unlike doctors, lawyers, teachers, social workers and so on, management qualifications have no state-backed professional registration which provides a license to practise, no defined or agreed body of knowledge, no monopoly over a specialist set of skills or tools. Universities and free-standing business schools have nobly stepped into this breach, producing a body of knowledge which is sufficiently vague and general, and then providing a range of qualifications to meet every budget.

When described like this, management is a very specific practice, a particular form of organizing that relies on hierarchy, inequalities of status and reward, and the reproduction of some remarkably vague forms of knowledge that suggest that management is the answer to every problem. The b-school is at the centre of this set-up, providing the cover-story that helps it to continue, and collecting a handsome stipend for doing so. We might almost think that no organizing could happen without management, so persuasive is the business school-industrial complex. How can anyone organize anything without managers? But management isn't the same as organization, as we will see in the next chapter.

7
The school for organizing

Revolt, the destruction of wealth, and social sabotage of the structures of power have in fact always been schools of organization.

(Hardt and Negri, *Commonwealth*)[1]

Hardt and Negri's point, as with much writing about social movements and revolutions, is that it is not only the powerful that organize. It would be understandable if we thought that was the case, because the structures of power are often enough giant institutions, enduring and highly visible sets of social relations, skyscrapers and palaces encased in stone and glass. This makes it look as if organizing is primarily a matter for government, corporations, universities – the places where we find managing, managers and management. Of course, these are forms of organizing, but the most important message of this book is that they are not the only forms of organizing, and that they are dwarfed by the sheer number of other ways in which organization can also happen, on other scales, through other means and for other purposes. People learn to organize, Hardt and Negri seem to be saying, outside and against the sorts of institutions represented by the b-school.

In 2016, a group of academics who were writing an attempt to justify something called the 'Business School Impact System' asked 'what would happen if business schools were to disappear?' It was a rhetorical question in one sense, since it was meant to propel the reader to an understanding of why it was so important that the 'Business School Impact System' was adopted, but their answer was: not much. Business schools, they said, are largely irrelevant to business, so the only people who would really notice would be students who were gainfully employed rather than paying fees and academics and administrators who would have to go and get proper jobs doing something productive.[2] Their paper was another rattle of the rigour/relevance 'debate', one that failed to ask who they should be relevant for, since the answer was so obvious already.

Let's take this suggestion seriously. How about shutting down the b-school, and opening schools for organizing?

EXCLUSIONS

As I suggested in Chapter 1, the sorts of doors to knowledge we find in universities are based on exclusions. A subject is made up by teaching this and not that, about space (geography) and not time (history), about collectives of people (sociology) and not about individuals (psychology), and so on. Of course there are leakages, and these are often where the most interesting thinking happens, but this partitioning of the world is constitutive of any university discipline. We cannot study everything, all the time, which is why there are names of departments over the doors to buildings and corridors.

However, the b-school is an even more extreme case. It is constituted through separating commercial life from the rest of life, but then undergoes a further specialization, a peristaltic contraction which squeezes out lots of other forms of organizing. As we saw in Chapter 2, the business school assumes capitalism, corporations and managers as the default form of organization, and everything else as history, anomaly, exception, alternative. In terms of curriculum and research, everything else is an option, not a core, something for the periphery, not the centre. Now (as we saw in Chapter 4), I am not the only person to have suggested that b-schools are obsessed with certain forms of organization, and that they tend to teach about corporations and free markets, that they are dominated by finance and that one step to improving matters might be to, as some commentators have suggested, 'take the business out of the b-school'.[3] It's a nice phrase but, as with most of those wailing about the sins of their employers, they don't say much about what that might mean. Just that 'something ought to be done', and that something usually requires the deployment of words like ethics, responsibility, morals and so on. But if we do want to take business out of the business school, or rather, want to expand the business school so that it wasn't only focused on one specific form of business, that wasn't only aimed at managers, why not begin by reconsidering the nature of the exclusions that have made this particular door to knowledge?

It is actually really easy to see that there are lots of forms of organization that an alternative 'School of Organizing'[4] might look at in order to learn lessons and teach about possibilities and problems. This means that the curriculum would not ignore organizations on a different scale, or in different cultures, or from different times, or that don't assume the capitalist economy. 'Organization' simply refers to patterns of people and things that humans arrange in order to get things done, the outcome of the patterning of people, technology and finance. It is a big word, a generous word, and it doesn't need to be reduced to 'management'. The etymology gives us the Latin *organa*, as an instrument or tool for a particular purpose, which in turn comes from *organon*, a Greek word which means something like 'that with which one works'. In English, the musical instrument and part of a body sense of 'organ' are both fifteenth century, as is the sense of organization (*organizationem*) as an action, as something that is done. It is not until the nineteenth century that the word solidifies into a thing, into an institution which is the precondition and/or consequence of a form of labour. The root of the word is some sort of device which effects a transformation, an arrangement which causes one thing to become something else. This is a productive notion and it implies a way of intervening in the world, of making the world different through the use of tools, of organs which produce a world which we can understand and work with.

To simplify considerably, organization, as a verb, produces organizations, as nouns.[5] The shape and size and durability of the nouns then mould the ways in which human beings can organize. We make institutions that shape us, and that shape our understanding of the world and our capacities to effect it. Studying how human beings organize, how they come together with each other and various non-human technologies, is therefore the subject matter of the school for organizing. Organizing is everywhere, and it varies according to degrees of formalization, visibility, stability and so on. It is a general verb which includes many specific processes, and a noun which covers multitudes of instances.

One way of expressing this would be a list of nouns then, a list of the outcomes of organizing processes. It could include co-operatives, local markets, kinship systems, groups, swaps, complementary or subaltern currencies, herds, networks, communes, clubs, worker self-management, pressure groups, partnerships, local exchange trading systems, hierarchies, democracies, councils, teams, bureaucracies, trusts, communities, time-banks, collectives, enterprises, professions, swarms, guilds, lineages, trade unions, states, clubs, occupations, social movements, solidarities and associations. That is to say, there are lots of different forms of organizing, and they all articulate different assumptions about hierarchy, economic exchange, tenure, boundaries and so on. Furthermore, they might be informed by anarchism, socialism, feminism, localism, libertarianism, environmentalism and whatever other complex politics human beings bring to bear on their lives. It does include conventional 'management' too of course, as well as 'markets', but only as two possibilities amongst many others.

The sorts of questions that the b-school asks tend to assume the sort of arrangements that it recognizes and prefers: 'Who are the managers?' 'How can the company be made more efficient?' 'How are you accounting for the profits?' 'What is the return for the shareholders?' If instead we ask, 'How are things organized?', we assume very little about what that particular arrangement looks like, beyond the idea that it is some sort of pattern that endures. Organizing is a general capacity for human beings, smart and sociable chimps who enjoy putting one thing on top of another. Asking about the ways in which human beings arrange and pattern their worlds is a general question, one that might be answered in different ways by any of the human sciences. It is a question that certainly might be answered by pointing to management, because that is a form of organization, but it's not the only one.

I suppose the general shape of the question we are then asking has both a factual and an exploratory element to it, 'How do people and things come together to do stuff?' That's an enquiry which would produce descriptions of the shapes of the worlds that human beings make here and now, and that could be enlarged by adding descriptions from other times and places. History, politics, geography, design and anthropology would be just as relevant as sociology and economics. The point of collecting such descriptions then also might become a kind of catalogue of possibilities, a bestiary of organizing, perhaps answering the question, 'How *can* people and things come together to do stuff?' Rather like a recipe book or toolbox, the catalogue doesn't tell us what we should do, but what humans can do, what we are capable of. Recipe books aren't instruction manuals, and you don't have to cook what they suggest in the way that they propose, but they are helpful if you have some ingredients and want to make something new, or to remind yourself of something that worked well in the past.

If we break the question down a little, we can come up with two different ways to understand it. First, if we ask about the organization of people, then the sorts of answers we get might be classified as technical matters pertaining to descriptions of the organization. This might involve size, structure, division of labour and specialization, use of material or virtual technologies, tenure of position, tenure of employment, decision-making structure, physical location of members, what can be expected for and from the worker, employee, or slave, employee ownership and raising of finance, nature of rules (informal or formal), assumptions about growth, assumptions about core business, distribution of profits or losses, accountability, relation to customers or clients, forms of co-ordination, degree of centralization or redundancy, extent of flexibility and so on. There are a lot of different variables here, because there are lots of different ways of being organized. As we have seen, the b-school tends to answer these questions in rather predictable ways, suggesting that, for example, bigger is better, hierarchies are always needed, decisions should be taken at the top, finance comes from investors, marketing is needed to persuade recalcitrant purchasers and so on.

We can add something else to this set of descriptions, because most forms of organization also come with a set of ideas and values which shape the exchange of things within and between organizations. So, we might then get answers about the organization of exchange which would describe who sells, who buys, who competes, what can be bought, sold, or exchanged, when and where, for how much or how little, under what rules, using what medium of exchange, with what information, derived from where, available to who and audited by who, with what assumptions about property rights, and to what end. Again, the business school tends to answer these questions in a very particular way, insisting that money is the only medium of exchange, information should be restricted to those at the apex of the organization, the aim of organizing is to generate profits, other organizations in the same business are competitors and so on.

So we have different ways of arranging human beings, and different ways of arranging exchange. Two variables, but each with lots of different possibilities. In a combinatorial spirit, if we then imagine putting these variables to work in order to complete the equation 'Organization + Exchange = X', our list of possibilities immediately becomes huge. We might imagine a list with descriptions of actual institutions such as families, stewarding, retail co-operatives, markets, kinship systems, groups, networks, communes, tribes, partnerships, local exchange trading systems, hierarchies, polyarchies, democracies, city-states, councils, teams, B-corps, bureaucracies, corporations, trusts, *Stiftung*, co-producers, monopolies, communities, autocracies, franchises, patriarchies, collectives, enterprises, sociocracies, NGOs, professions, family businesses, lineages, monopsonies, institutions, trade unions, states, companies, councils, governments, clubs, cultures, worker co-operatives, totalitarian regimes, occupations, societies, foundations, social enterprises, holarchies, matriarchies, solidarities, associations, *Waqf*, charities, non-profits, villages, sects, phalanxes, credit unions, provident or mutual societies and hybrids of all the above. This is not an infinite list, because it is limited by what human beings have done so far and what we can find out about it, but just imagining it gives us an idea of the variability of ways in which us clever chimps have arranged our worlds.

The business school cannot describe, or perhaps even understand, this diversity, because its is already committed to the narrow idea of market managerialism. Like a medical school that only teaches about arms and legs, it doesn't even consider most forms of organization as relevant to its research and teaching.

Even small deviations from this ideal type show us how partial the view from the business school really is.

SUMA

Let's just take one example: Suma Foods, a worker co-operative incorporated as an industrial and provident society, that is to say, an organization owned and run by its members. It was founded in the northern English city of Leeds in 1977 and is the largest independent wholefood wholesaler in the United Kingdom, specializing in vegetarian, organic, ethical and natural products. In 2016, this particular co-operative was one of 6,797 co-ops in the UK, which overall employ a total of 222,785 people, and with a turnover of £35.7 billion.[6] Co-ops are a substantial part of this particular national economy, not a marginal decoration.

Suma was started in 1975 by Reg Tayler. Tayler had already gained some experience of wholefoods and retailing in London, and when he moved to Leeds he opened a retail shop, Plain Grain. In August 1975, at a meeting attended by other wholefood shops in the north of England, he proposed they set up a wholesaling co-operative in order to supply each other. Reg and friends set up in the back kitchen of a house in Leeds from where they sold cereal flakes, dried fruits and brown rice. They soon needed more room, and so rented a lock-up garage nearby – this is where the name 'Suma' was first used for the business. Within a year they needed larger premises, and in 1976 acquired a warehouse. In 1977, Tayler sold the Suma business to the then seven employees, who became the founder members of the 'Triangle Wholefoods Collective', trading as Suma. Rapid expansion of the wholefood market meant that by 1986 Suma had moved to a larger warehouse in Halifax, 14 miles away. Alongside the growth in size, there was a corresponding increase in the complexity and sophistication of the business, and the structure of the co-op went through many modifications to manage this change. In 2001, Suma moved to purpose-built premises in nearby Elland.

By the 1980s, Suma had become the hub of a cluster of spin-off co-operatives in the food sector including 'Beano Wholefoods' (a retailer which lasted from 1978 to 2007), 'Hebden Water Milling Collective' (which mixed and packaged food and produced nut butters, but was deregistered in 1999) and 'Cena' (a research co-op). It was also a major customer of the Wharf Street Café and collaborated with Leeds Beer Co-operative. For a period of several years in the 1980s, each time members decided to increase the pay rate, the same amount was put into the co-operative development fund. This method of expansion was based on the creation of independent co-operative businesses, not growth of the core organization. Indeed, at this time, Suma deliberately devolved several of its regional markets, such as Scotland and the East Midlands, to other co-ops.

All the products are vegetarian, from sweets to toothbrushes. That means no meat, no fish and no animal-derived products like gelatin or rennet. Where eggs are an ingredient, they are free-range. Suma stock organic versions of everything they can, support fair trade as a licensee of the Fairtrade Foundation and all their bodycare, cosmetic and household products are cruelty-free. Suma's commitment to fair trade is not a marketing device; it is one based on a deeply held belief in a universal right to economic justice, self-empowerment and freedom from exploitation. They are also acutely aware of the impact that business has on the environment at local and global levels and hence try to keep carbon emissions to a minimum. Suma use 100 per cent renewable electricity and motion sensors in rooms to switch the lights off when there is no activity. Sales representatives share a hybrid car, and their trucks use vehicle tracking to reduce mileage. They take back plastic and cardboard packaging from customers and what they are unable to re-use, they recycle. Food waste is composted, they plant enough trees to get carbon-neutral status, and have appointed a carbon champion to monitor the organization's footprint.

So far so good, but most importantly for my purposes here, Suma is a workers' co-operative, which means that the business is jointly owned and controlled by all the workers. Everyone is paid the same – in 2016, that was £40 000 a year for the 161 permanent members and over £11 an hour for temporary workers. Job rotation is simply assumed, with everyone collectively doing all the jobs that need doing, whatever they happen to be and regardless of status. Jenny Carlyle, Suma member and personnel officer, says that

> ... very few people do the same job five days a week and most will also do some warehouse jobs in the week, so something like picking, or loading trucks, or working in the fridges or freezers. You can imagine what a nightmare it would be to say 'you're on one rate for picking in the warehouse, you're on another for being a member of the sales team.' Working out how to pay people for a week's work would be impossible.[7]

This sort of multi-skilling also enables collaborative democratic decision making, as all members have at least some experience of every area, and therefore practical knowledge on which to base discussion and decisions. Underpinning all this is the expectation that members will 'self-manage', as Carlyle says:

> Self-management is written into our job descriptions and how we train new members. We encourage everybody to ask questions, whether they're here as a short-term worker, whether they have a lot of experience or are fresh out of university ... and people are pretty good at finding the information they need to inform themselves.

The insistence on equal pay is the most obvious way of showing that all work in the organization is valuable, with workers never having to wonder how their pay compares with that of someone else. Jenny Carlyle again:

> Picking the orders would be the lowest-paid job in a similar company but actually that's our core business: if we didn't have that we wouldn't have the rest, so it shows we value all of the inputs to the business equally. Pay is only ever on the table when we're discussing whether or not to give ourselves a pay rise, so it takes away that hassle – everyone knows where they stand.

In some ways, Suma is an unremarkable company. It buys, sells and moves a set of products that customers want. There is nothing particularly innovative about the core aspects of their business model, involving trucks and a warehouse. However, as is clear from the above, the way that they run the business denies hierarchical organization, and refuses a permanent division of labour, asymmetries of knowledge and reward, the externalization of costs, and even assumptions about growth. Members of Suma assume that the organizing principal is 'self-management', not management by managers. This is a company which is clearly driven by idealism, with a vision of a different world, but which also deals with practical questions in ways that have been making its members a good living for over forty years.

SCHOOLING ORGANIZING

I simply want to use the example above to show that there are viable alternatives to management as a general form of organizing. Suma is just one relatively small company, one co-op among nearly 7,000 others in the UK at the time of writing, but it is an example that can be used to question many of the core assumptions of contemporary management ideas. It shows that a different combination of organization plus exchange can work and last, can combine idealism with practicality. And if we had space, we could add to this catalogue, this bestiary, by describing other arrangements that challenge the conventions of managerialism in the name of democracy, equality, sustainability and more.

Because the point is not that all organizations should be like Suma. The idea of generalized models that can be transferred regardless of local circumstances is one that schools of business often sell. Instead, it seems to me that the point of exploring alternatives is to open up diversity, to encourage reflection on the sheer variety of ways in which human beings can come together and solve the collective problems that they face. The most important issue to address does not concern particular models and the choices between them, but a recognition that organizing is a political and ethical matter. This means that management ideas, or rather, ideas about organization, embed assumptions about the relationship between human beings and things – they are politics made durable.

And this includes the School of Organizing itself. Indeed, the paradox of institutionalization is built into the very idea. As Hardt and Negri imply, their school of organizing exists in life, in the ways in which people resist, cope and arrange their lives within and against the structures of power. The idea of making such an idea into an institution is something of a problem then, because it sets in stone that which has been declared to be fluid, resulting in a premature case of sclerosis, of the determination (in advance) of what is to be found behind the oak-panelled doorway to knowledge. More of this later, but for now, a few remarks on how the schooling might be imagined, paying particular attention to the importance of this being a place and time which is open, in which the door is ajar.

First, it is important to acknowledge the domination of the Anglo world, of the English language and of a very particular kind of history. The school for organizing would have to be open, to continually and consciously open itself, to other traditions, disciplines, contexts.[8] This is not just a matter of being inclusive, or even politically correct, but rather a precondition of being able to do what it needs to do. If its mission is to study organizing, then it needs to be capable of soliciting examples from everywhere; otherwise it will be restricting its objects of enquiry in ways that will prevent it from being able to achieve its mission. If a scientist, intending to study a particular phenomenon, decided in advance that they would only study it at a certain temperature or pressure, but without good reason, then they would not be doing good science. Restrictions are necessary to produce domains of enquiry, but once those domains have been broadly applied, further limits would usually be understood to be either experimental conditions which had been reflected upon or bad experimental design. In other words, if the school wants to only teach and research 'organizing by capitalists in the Global North', or 'organizing by the middle classes', it would need to say so, and face whatever consequences follow.

In part, this is a gamble on how a 'proper' science, or academic subject should operate. As I suggested earlier, we would be suspicious of a biology department which only studied animals with fur, or refused to include plants that weren't green. The wager here is that the legitimacy of science, and of the idea of the university itself, means that the school for organizing will have to be inclusive rather than exclusive. In other words, if there are exclusions, they will need to be marked, or treated as experimental conditions to be addressed at some future date. Sumantra Ghoshal, in his splendid tirade against the current dominance within the b-school of the 'gloomy ideology' that assumes self-interest, tries something similar. He notes that this is effectively to assume that we already know what human beings are like, and how they will behave, when he believes that this should be treated as an open question. To drop these 'neoliberal' assumptions would, he says, result in a more scientific approach, an approach which attempts to discard preconceptions in order to see the object of enquiry with as much clarity as possible.[9] The idea of the university as a safe harbour for science is here being used as a bulwark against ideology, against the idea that we already know the answers, and hence already know the questions too.

This leads into the second issue, which is that the school for organizing would need to be an interdisciplinary place. Now we know that this is always a problem for universities, and for academics, because the very structure of the university, of the architecture of committees and journals, as well as that of buildings, makes staying apart much easier than coming together. Nonetheless, and following the general line above, since we can't delineate in advance the limits of what it means to study forms of organizing, then history, geography, and social anthropology are obvious resources for investigating other times, places and people. This doesn't mean that the school for organizing would be indistinguishable from these subjects, but it does suggest that a sensible approach to such research and teaching ambitions would not begin with a restriction to contemporary organizing in the Global North. In any case, the insights of sociologists and political theorists will be relevant to such matters, particularly with regard to a sensitivity to the ways that gender, class, ethnicity and their intersections might figure in organizing, and the forms that political organizing takes place outside 'political' institutions.

The social sciences aren't the only places to look of course, because, as several of the nostalgic critics we reviewed in Chapter 4 have suggested, the cultivation of imagination and character are also part of the remit of the school for organizing. Particularly because those who do so are likely to be the sort of people who have some influence in the world. In a rare and nice essay on how the business school might be reformed, two b-school academics described their hopes for a revived business school as somewhere for 'the study, stimulation, and design of new forms of responsible and creative collective action'.[10] Just as examples of organizing will need to be sourced from as many places as possible, it seems to me that creativity and responsibility will require the sort of imaginative engagement that might be provided from studies of art and the humanities, as well as methods for studying and understanding that are based on close readings of literature, films, Internet media and so on. Again, this is not to say that the school for organizing will become a cultural studies or history of art department, but to insist that it should be continually open to ideas, sources and methods from other places. After all, if you assume that you never know what you will find, and where you might find it, then the world becomes open to you. Much of what you find may not be useful, and will be forgotten or become decoration that gathers dust, but some of it will be diamonds.

The last way in which I want to gesture to this openness is to return to the continuing question of whether this is a school within the university or an outpost of the world. The rigour and relevance debate is a displaced echo of this question, though it largely assumes that we already know what rigour is and who we are trying to be relevant for. It seems to me that there is no single answer to this 'inside' or 'outside' question, because the terms are parasitic on each other. Rather as Kant suggested, there will never be a reconciliation between the lower and higher faculties, because they lean against each other, they define each other, as well as both being necessary for a desirable world. In one of the more interesting books on the business school, the authors suggest that it should be an agora not a campus, a place where people come to debate,[11] not somewhere to hide away from the world. That is a rather an either/or formulation, but it does contain the idea that the school is a space into which people travel, and within which deliberations and arguments will happen. This requires that it is partly separated from the world, in order that it has some distance from it, as well as being open to and responsible for that world, in order that its discussions have some meaning beyond a small community of dusty scholars, compiling their reference books and throwing paper planes at each other while muttering.

AN ENDLESS CATALOGUE

Over a decade ago, I and some colleagues approached a publisher with a proposal for a *Dictionary of Alternatives*.[12] It was to have lots of short entries and cross-references, just like a proper dictionary should have. The idea was that this would be a catalogue of possibilities, a gigantic interconnecting list of ideas, practices and institutions. Not just 'actual' ones either, but also dreams, plans and possibilities – intentional communities and utopian literature – particularly those that had been inspired by, or had themselves inspired, people doing things in the world. It was meant to be the sort of book that might be grazed upon for inspiration whilst on the toilet or train, but was also intended to be a disguised polemic, or even art-work, in which 'management' and 'business' were merely items in a much longer list. They were to be put in their place, so to speak, one option amongst many. No big deal.

The publishers agreed, and we set to work. The book grew, with entries multiplying like rhizomatic rabbits, spawning new lines of enquiry into seventeenth-century utopian fiction, hierarchical choirs of angels, criminal organizations, political strategies, different co-operative businesses and networks, secret societies, charismatic dreamers and prophets, the cellular organization of terrorist groups. My office was covered with piles of paper, categories, lists, themes. But it had to stop eventually, because other matters were pressing, and we ended up with a manuscript which had around a quarter of a million words. On presenting this to the publishers, an animated discussion ensued, because they had agreed to publish a book of 80,000 words and something this large just wouldn't work. It wasn't economically possible. Eventually we compromised, with some bitterness, at 120,000, and so the scissors and red pencil started to fly. Whole branches of enquiry were lopped and pruned, and enough words for another entire book hit the dust.[13]

After the bitterness had subsided, I still thought that what was left was remarkable. A crazy mosaic of connections and jumps, a tree that was dense in some places and sparse in others, a curriculum for a School of Organizing perhaps, but still a shadow of what it could have been, which in turn was a shadow of some other even larger compendium which impossibly attempted to document the massive creativity of human beings when they come together with others in order to do stuff. An imaginary library, informed by the past but stretching into the future.

Here is the list of contents from the published book, so that you can see all the things that didn't end up on the cutting room floor, or that we decided not to include, or that we didn't even know about because the book was written by Europeans in English. Warning, it's still a big list …

ABBEY OF THELEME, ACTION DIRECTE, AGORA, ALTERNATIVE GEOPOLITICS, ALTERNATIVE TECHNOLOGY, See APPROPRIATE TECHNOLOGY, AMAZONS, AMERICA, AMISH, ANARCHISM, ANDRAE, Johann Valentin, See CHRISTIANOPOLIS, ANGRY BRIGADE, ANTI-CAPITALISM, ANTI-GLOBALISATION, See ANTI-CAPITALISM, ANTI-UTOPIA, See DYSTOPIA, APPROPRIATE TECHNOLOGY, ARCADIA, ARISTOPHANES, ARIZMENDIARRIETA, JOSÉ MARIA, See MONDRAGON, ARTS AND CRAFTS, ATLANTIS, ATTAC, AUROVILLE, AUTO-DIDACTICISM, AUTONOMIA, AUTONOMOUS WORKING GROUPS, See KALMAR, QUALITY OF WORKING LIFE, BAADER-MEINHOF GROUP, See RED ARMY FACTION, BACK-TO-THE-LANDERS, See SUBSISTENCE WORK,

BACON, Francis, See NEW ATLANTIS, BAKUNIN, MIKHAIL, BALL, John, BARTERING, BATTLE OF SEATTLE, BELLAMY, Edward, See LOOKING BACKWARD, BEN & JERRY, BLAC(K) BLOC, BLACK PANTHER PARTY, BLAKE, William, BODY SHOP, BOOKCHIN, Murray, BOURNVILLE, BOYCOTT, BRETHREN OF THE FREE SPIRIT, BRIGATE ROSSI, See RED BRIGADES, BROOK FARM, BUDDHIST MONASTICISM, BUREAUCRACY, BUTLER, Samuel, See EREWHON, CABET, Etienne, See VOYAGE TO ICARIA, CADBURY, See BOURNVILLE, CAMPANELLA, Giovan Domenico (Thomasso), See CITY OF THE SUN, CAPTAIN SWING, CARNIVAL, CASTRO, Fidel (1927–), CATHARS, CELEBRATION, CENTRI SOCIALI, CHIPKO MOVEMENT, CHRISTIANIA, CHRISTIANOPOLIS, CITY OF THE SUN, CITY-STATE, CIVIL DISOBEDIENCE, See GANDHI; WALDEN, COCKAIGNE (Or Cockaygne), COHN-BENDIT, Daniel, CO-HOUSING, See CO-OPERATIVE, COLLECTIVISM, COMMONWEALTH, COMMUNE, COMMUNISM, COMMUNITARIANISM, COMMUNITY, Community Credit, COMMUNITY CURRENCY, See BARTERING, LOCAL EXCHANGE TRADING SCHEMES, TIME BANKS, Community Garden, COMMUNITY SUPPORTED AGRICULTURE, COMTE, Auguste, CONDORCET, Marie-Jean-Antoine-Nicholas De Caritat, Marquis De, COOPERATIVE CITY, CO-OPERATIVES, CORBUSIER, See LE CORBUSIER, CREDIT UNION, CRUSOE, See ROBINSON CRUSOE, CUBA, CULT, DE FOIGNY, See NEW DISCOVERY OF TERRA INCOGNITA AUSTRALIS, DE SADE, See DE SADE, DEFOE, See ROBINSON CRUSOE, DEMOCRACY, DEMOCRATIC SCHOOL, See SUDBURY VALLEY SCHOOL, SUMMERHILL, DIDEROT, See SUPPLEMENT TO BOUGAINVILLE'S VOYAGE, DIGGERS, DIRECT ACTION, DISOBBEDIENTI, DISPOSSESSED, The, DISSENTING ACADEMIES,

Sidney, WEBER, Max, see bureaucracy; cults, WELLS, H. G,
William Godwin, Winstanley, Gerrard, WOMAN ON THE
EDGE OF TIME, Worker Self-Management, Works Councils,
ZAPATISTAS.

You will know something about some of those words, but probably
not all of them, and that in itself is an invitation for study. The
list contains mysteries, and that seems a pretty good start for
the sorts of things that might be taught and researched within
the School of Organizing. At least, it's a start, because there was
an awful lot missing, such as Suma and the organization of the
school for organizing itself.

But next, how do we choose from this catalogue? After all, this
is just a list, it's not a curriculum, or a series of classified examples
of particular problems and solutions. Are all forms of organizing
equally good, or bad?

8

The politics of organizing

'Don't mourn, organize!'
Joe Hill[1]

[handwritten annotation: Cunning Plan]

The argument in the previous chapter is a cunning one. It has two elements. One is to say that universities should study everything in their subject area, that chemists should not decide that chlorine is not on the syllabus. If the business school wants to be a proper discipline, and not just an ideologically driven finishing school, then co-operatives and segmentary lineage systems should be as important as corporations and management. The other part of the argument is really just a list, a dizzying catalogue of difference that reminds us that human beings have organized themselves, animals, devices, symbols and the environment in some astonishing ways. Come and explore!

Human beings are organizing animals. Through language and socio-technical arrangements, they build worlds to live in, and the baroque complexity of these worlds is what distinguishes them from the other creatures on earth. What we know of human history and physical and social anthropology tells us that the variety of these human-made worlds has been spectacular. Bloody temples to sacrifice, secret organizations that hide their very existence, kings with the power to erase life with the flick of a pen, circles of gift giving with sea shells across chains of islands, nomads following migrations of animals, glittering cities with towers nearly a mile high, ceremonies involving particular sorts of food prepared and served quietly in houses made from paper.

A science fiction catalogue of permutations, of fantastic worlds known and unknown, of teeming forms of life which endlessly mutate into shades of horror and violence, as well as beauty and generosity.

And that's the problem. The invitation to study the list, to snuffle around in the dictionary of alternatives, appears to come without any political or ethical strings attached. The dictionary doesn't tell us which arrangements are better or worse, which form of organizing crushes people, and which leaves them starving. Floating over the terrain, we can survey diversity and difference with magisterial fascination, but without getting encumbered by judgements. The list is just butterfly collecting, a rag-bag or rattle-bag of this and that, with no ways of classifying the variety, no taxonomies of type or problem or interest. It allows us to see things but without getting entangled in the joys and pains of others, and without expressing any preference for this sort of world rather than that one, for this kind of organization, and not that one.

The paradox, or contradiction, is that I am criticizing the b-school for being an institution that has a hidden curriculum which is based on excluding pretty much anything that isn't managed capitalism, but my response so far has stayed at pluralism, at the injunction to let a thousand flowers bloom. In this chapter, I want to show why that isn't really enough, because it seems to me that the school for organizing cannot be agnostic about such matters. Fascism, feudalism, slavery and the mafia are ways of organizing, and they should be considered as such, but the school for organizing should also be providing ways to think about the political and ethical questions that might be asked about any particular form of organizing.

There are many 'alternatives' to the present, but I do not think that they are all equally good. So in this chapter I'm going to begin by thinking about politics, in order to clarify just how organizations can be seen as a form of politics made durable, as a decision about the relationship between means and ends. I'm going to suggest three broad orientations, values, logics, or principles which might help us think about how what sorts of alternatives we might consider from the catalogue of possibilities that face us. This, it seems to me, should be the proper task of a school for organizing.

THE POLITICS OF MEANS AND ENDS

It would be hard to say that there are any forms of organization, or specific organizations, which we can always and forever decide are good.[2] There are plenty of accounts of institutions which start well, but fall into bad habits, or become dominated by a cadre of leaders, or within which the excitement of the new becomes the atrophy of the old. Sometimes we could say that a noble goal has been displaced by the logic of capitalism. Another possible explanation is that, as the sociologist Robert Michels suggested with his phrase the 'iron law of oligarchy',[3] those who become powerful within an organization are often motivated by self-preservation, glorification and the consolidation of power, or if they are not like that, they become so. This means that organizations often just keep on doing whatever it is that they do, like zombies that stagger on but have no consciousness or heart.

We always need to be wary about organizing, even organizing that looks like it is 'alternative'. Part of the problem here rests on making some judgements about the inseparability of means and ends. That is to say, is it enough to decide that a particular form of organizing aims at an end that we deem to be 'good'? We might well say that it is, and consequently that certain ends justify almost any means. So, if a corporation is making money from selling cheap clothing, but people in the Global South are being paid above market rates to make it, then we might be satisfied. Or, if a very hierarchical form of managerialism is being used in a company that manufactures organic foods, then we could still potentially agree that this is a good organization. Of course we can also play these arguments in reverse, and suggest that the means are the evidence that we should use in our judgements. So if an egg producer was co-operatively owned and managed, but engaged in a particularly cruel form of factory farming, we might discount the means and focus on the discomfort to the chickens. Or perhaps we could imagine a form of community currency being used to exclude 'outsiders' from engaging in certain kinds of financial transactions. In these cases, it might be that our care for animals, or for a certain sort of human, means that the ownership of the organization or the origin of the medium of exchange is pretty irrelevant to our final judgements.

It is obvious that the distinctions we are making here are very troublesome, and could well create some rather paradoxical outcomes. I think that any argument about a separation between means and ends should be treated with extreme scepticism, because you cannot make a judgement about one in isolation from the other. The distinction between the two often makes us assume that we have no choice but to use particular methods, or to attempt to achieve particular goals. Think about the idea of making a decision. Within corporate organizations, decisions are made by those with power and status. We could say that a decision is a means to an end, and having 'managers' to make those decisions is a means that ensures that getting to the end is more speedy and efficient. Perhaps, but as many radicals have argued, we could treat a collective form of decision making as an end in itself, as an art of co-operating, and not simply a way of getting things done. If the intention of the organization's members is to take decisions slowly and democratically, then the very process of organizing in a particular way becomes its own reward, as well as a way in which other goals might be achieved. As work on the alter-globalization movement shows, such organizing is 'prefigurative' in the sense that it attempts to bring new forms of social relationships into being. A distinction between means and end, cause and effect, which seems quite secure in common sense begins to look rather suspicious, and politically loaded, in the context of alternative organizing which attempts to build horizontal social relations in the shadow of an either/or logic.[4]

So I am suspicious of arguments which suggest that any means are acceptable to achieve certain ends, just as I am about suggestions that only certain means are 'efficient' or justifiable. If a corporation donates money to a homelessness charity in the name of corporate social responsibility, but it has generated this money (and much more) by exploiting offshored low-wage labour, then it might seem that the end somehow makes the means legitimate. Being wary about this set-up is not to say that I am against the reduction of homelessness, simply that I do not think that any means are justifiable. (And in any case, there might be better means than these.) This argument shows that we can, and should, treat all arguments about means and ends as political ones. We should always be suspicious if someone – perhaps someone in a b-school – tells that there is no alternative, no choice, and that we should be 'realistic'. The end point of many arguments against change is that things have to be like this because of 'the market', or 'the bottom line', or 'human nature' which are usually assertions that suit those who have something to defend in the present state of affairs. In fact, no particular forms of human organizing are inevitable and there are always choices about means, ends, and the relations between them. They might not be easy choices, but they are choices.

AUTONOMY, CO-OPERATION AND THE FUTURE

Opening up the politics and possibilities of organizing as a way of contesting the hegemony of the b-school doesn't solve our problems. It makes things much more difficult because we can no longer admit of any arguments about inevitability, and instead have to justify our individual and collective choices on the basis of what forms of life we wish to encourage. These will have to be reasons which encompass both means and ends, processes and purposes, and rest upon some sort of idea about the kinds of society and people we believe to be desirable. This means that visions of a better form of social order, ideas about utopia if you like, are central to the judgements we might make concerning what is alternative and what is mainstream, about the difference between fair exchange and appropriation, generosity and corporate social responsibility. We cannot assume that we will ever know the 'one best way' to organize (to borrow Frederick Taylor's term), and might instead encourage debate about ideas that are different to the way that we do things now – whether old, new, marginal, hidden, possible, or imaginary. Something like the dictionary in the previous chapter is a sourcebook for these discussions.

Having said that, it seems necessary to try to explore some general principles, because I am not suggesting that 'anything goes'. Instead, I think there are three broad orientations, values, logics, or principles that should be at work in our discussion of alternatives – autonomy, solidarity and responsibility – and in this section I will explore them in a bit more detail. Note that what I am doing here is making normative statements about what I think should be desirable features of a different world, because I do not think that this world, whatever the b-school suggests, is an inevitable one. Other worlds are possible.

First, I think that any alternative worth exploring must be able to protect some fairly conventional notions of individual autonomy, that is to say, to respect ourselves. This is not a controversial or novel idea, but one that underpins most conservative, liberal and libertarian political philosophy.[5] Words like 'liberty', 'diversity', 'dignity' and 'difference' are more often honoured in the breach rather than the observance, but still gesture towards the radical proposal that individual freedoms really do matter. When we feel that we have been forced to do something that we don't want to do, we are diminished in an important way, and any social system which relies on coercion of an economic, ideological or physical form is not one which we can support easily. This means that I do think that individuals should have choices about some of the most important ways in which they live their lives. If there is no autonomy within a given social system, only rules, then we are justified in calling it totalitarian, uniform and intolerant of difference. For most people, this will be an easy principle to establish, because it underlies so much of the ideology which supports neoliberal capitalism, and yet I also want to argue that it contains a radical core which must lie at the heart of any robust 'alternative'.

My second principle reverses the assumptions of the first, and begins with the collective, and our duties to others. This could be variously underpinned with forms of communist, socialist and communitarian thought, as well as virtue ethics, and insists that we are social creatures who are necessarily reliant on others.[6] This means that words like 'solidarity', 'co-operation', 'community' and 'equality' become both descriptions of the way that human beings are, and prescriptions for the way that they should be. On their own, human beings are vulnerable and powerless, victims of nature and circumstance. Collectively – bound together by language, culture and organization – they become powerful, and capable of turning the world to their purposes. Perhaps even more important than this is the way in which we humans actually make each other, providing the meanings and care which allow us to recognize ourselves as ourselves through the eyes of others. In the most general sense, this is what 'social construction' means: the making of the human through and with other humans in such a way that it becomes impossible to imagine even being human without some conception of a society to be oriented to.

Let's pause a moment before thinking about the third principle, because it's fairly clear that one and two are at best in tension with one another, at worst contradictory. How can we be both true to ourselves, and at the same time orient ourselves to the collective? How can we value freedom, but then give it up to the group? The answer is that we need to understand both principles as co-produced. For example, when we speak of being free, we usually mean 'free to', in the sense of being free to be able to exercise choices about where to go, who to vote for, what to buy and so on. This is precisely the idea of liberty that we are very often encouraged to imagine as being the pre-eminent value around which our lives *should* be organized within a consumer society, the sort of society that the b-school describes. But a moment's thought also allows us to see that 'freedom to' is only possible if we also experience 'freedom from'. As the political philosopher Isaiah Berlin put it, 'positive' and 'negative' liberty are not the same things, even if they appear to be aimed at the same goals.[7] The individual freedom to be who we want to be rests on our freedoms from hunger, dislocation, violence and so on, which can only be pursued collectively. We, as individuals, can only exercise our autonomy within some sort of collective agreement, a social contract if you like, which provides us with a shelter against events. So 'freedom' is an entirely abstract concept unless it is embedded within some sort of social organization. Otherwise, we might as well talk about being free to be paid low wages by a corporation, or to work in monotonous jobs, or at liberty to become a refugee or political prisoner. This is what liberalism, and extreme libertarianism, so often miss. In its entirely credible and modern defence of individual autonomy against despotic exercises of power, liberalism tends to have an allergic reaction towards the institutions which are needed to ensure that we can eat well and sleep safely in our beds.

The reverse is also true of course. As the history of the twentieth century showed very clearly, just because a social system claims to be collective (whether communist, nationalist, capitalist, or national socialist), it doesn't mean that it represents all of us all of the time. Even if it is supported by a majority, there might be compelling reasons not to support certain dominant norms, to stand out against the mass. Often enough, loud claims to be representing others are actually providing a warrant for the powerful to do what they want. The suggestion that individual preferences should always be dissolved in the collective, and that any dissent from the dominant line is heretical, is one that we find in a wide variety of flavours. Liberty is usually suppressed in the name of a greater good – 'the company', 'the people', 'the state', 'the nation' – but what is common is that it requires conformity, fear, exile, or death to enforce it. There is not such a merit in being collective that the destruction of all autonomy is necessary in order to achieve it. Indeed, as the sociologist Zygmunt Bauman has argued, the impulse to create the perfect collectivity is itself something to be distrusted.[8] The idea of creating the ideal human within the ideal city is one that requires that people and things which don't fit are 'weeded' out, and that all the contradictions and politics of real people in real places are dealt with through a form of social engineering. It is because of such assumptions – often enough wielded by chief executives and their human resource officers – that assertions of individual liberty matter.

That being said, the dichotomy between the individual and society is not quite so straightforward or dramatic, because it is also often mediated by some sort of identity as a member of a group, class, or category *within* or *between* wider societies. When organizing happens on this level – social movements, women's groups, indigenous organizations, social class–based politics – it is often protecting a form of collective autonomy against perceived repression or ignorance. The politics of identity insists on the importance of some form of collective distinctions and on the 'right' to express them. Here we can see many practical examples of how a certain sort of individual difference becomes aligned with a co-operative strategy, and consequently a form of distinctiveness can be articulated as the precondition for a form of solidarity. When a group of anarchists establish their own co-operative, or migrants establish some sort of mutual financial organization, they are making an identity claim. We can be 'different together', a position which appears to dissolve a clear distinction between liberalism and communitarianism, between the demand for freedom and the embracing of a collectivity. This is not the same as insisting on radical autonomy, but neither is it necessarily a form of totalitarianism. As with many matters, the messy reality of actual organizing is rarely as simple as neat theoretical distinctions would suggest. The anarchist Mikhail Bakunin expressed it with pithy clarity – 'we are convinced that liberty without socialism is privilege, injustice; and that socialism without liberty is slavery and brutality.'[9]

In any case, even if we acknowledge that our two first principles do embody a profound if necessary contradiction, does this matter? Contradiction is not something to be feared or eliminated, as if the 'one best way' could be described once and for all. Instead, it is a lived reality for people who take on the responsibilities of organizing people and things, as they juggle mixed motives and outcomes individually and collectively. The tensions between being free, making enough money, having an impact, worrying about the future or whatever, are not ones which will go away by making theoretical gestures. Indeed, if there were no tensions or conflicts in a particular set of ideas, it would be difficult to understand it as living thought. If we already have all the answers, if we already know that corporations are the most effective way to arrange the world, then there would be little point in debating alternatives and no way to understand what a word like 'politics' might mean.

My third principle is a little easier, however, in the sense that it presents a more direct challenge to the externalizing tendencies of corporate capitalism. I think that any alternative worth the name must have a responsibility to the future – to the conditions for our individual and collective flourishing. Edmund Burke put it rather nicely, in his 1790 *Reflections on the Revolution in France*, suggesting that society 'is a partnership ... not only between those who are living, but between those who are living, those who are dead, and those who are to be born.'[10] This will involve words which are used often in b-schools nowadays, but not always taken very seriously as practices, such as sustainability, accountability, stewarding, development and progress. The economic and organizational structures of the present tend not to encourage such responsibilities, instead treating people and planet as resources which can be used for short-term gain by a few. In large part, these are matters which bear upon questions of climate change, environmental degradation and loss of biodiversity, but not exclusively. The conditions for our individual and collective flourishing are also institutional and cultural, and hence any responsibility to the future must also have regard to the sorts of people we create, and the sort of organizational arrangements that they make, and that make them. This means, for example, being attentive to what technologies do to us and for us; what sort of assumptions about democracy and hierarchy we embed into our workplaces; or how we imagine people can own organizations, and hence other people's labour. I take 'responsibility' to be a term which presses us to think about all sorts of consequences, which encourages us to respond to the 'long future', and not insulate ourselves with the usual arguments which merely end up displacing problems to some other place, and some other time. As the Great Law of the Iroquois Confederacy was supposed to have it – 'In every deliberation, we must consider the impact of our decisions on the next seven generations.'[11]

What we have here then are three principles which I think the school for organizing should ask its students to discuss, three responsibilities which must be negotiated and understood – to ourselves, to others, and to our future. All three are important, and any one in isolation is insufficient. An organization which only defends individual liberty will not be able to co-ordinate very much, but an organization which ruthlessly demands collective loyalty must necessarily expel disagreement. And, since we don't know and probably won't agree on what the future should look like, then the balance between individualism and collectivism will also be written across our futures. These three cannot be treated as matters that can ever be solved for once and for all, but rather as concerns that must be raised, and addressed, in the certain knowledge that there will always be disagreements. Too much concern for ourselves ends up as possessive individualism and selfishness; too much direction from others and bending to the collective will is a form of coercion, and too many promises about the ideal future neglect the mucky problems of the present. All three are necessary, but all three are entangled and in practice may well be contradictory. But then who said politics was easy?

ORGANIZING AS POLITICS

I have suggested three broad ways in which we might judge forms of organization for their politics, but why does this matter? Well, I believe that thinking about these three dimensions makes organization into a series of choices and encourages us to see that there is always another way of getting things done. It problema-tizes the relationship between means and ends, often making means into ends themselves. Rather than believing that 'we have no alternative', we become able to see that 'organizing' is an open process, and become more able to understand and debate the values which underpin particular institutions and ways of doing things.

Another implication of this is to think of organizing as a kind of politics made durable,[12] as the sedimentation of conventions and expectations in organization charts and payscales. An organization might not look like politics, but it functions like a mould, shaping the ways that thinking and action can happen. The dominant business school versions of corporations, markets, management, hierarchy, leaders, employees, consumption and so on constitute a particular set of historical, legal and political assumptions. These aren't necessary and inevitable arrangements, dictated by the structure of our monkey genetics, or the calculus of the invisible hand of the market. Rather than seeing organizing as a technical matter, something to be left to experts with MBAs perhaps, we can understand it as a way of working through the complex ways of being human with other humans and hence a responsibility and possibility for all of us. This encourages what we might call 'prefigurative organization' – 'reflexive organizing', or 'meta-organizing' – a form of working which deliberately and continually reflects on how people and things are being put together.

For example, if we claim that democracy – the rule of the people – is a value that we care about then we might reasonably ask just why so many decisions in workplaces are taken autocratically, by a small minority. Arguments from expertise or efficiency might work in particular cases – such as when a doctor uses their expertise to diagnose a medical problem, or something must be done quickly – but this is not the case in many situations. Why assume that all forms of organization need a class of people called 'managers', and that these people should be paid so much more than the workers? Why are these managers appointed, and not elected? Why assume that the people who work for a company will be different to the people who own it? Why not have workers or trade union representatives sitting on boards of directors? Why do shareholders have votes, but not employees, members of local communities, customers and so on? Why does shareholder return matter more than the environment, or the pay and conditions of workers, or the lies that you tell customers?

Once these sorts of questions and many others are opened up, it is difficult to get them back in the box. The answers become prefigurative of a certain attitude, a constitutive and practical politics in themselves. This is to stress the open-ended quality of organizing and the importance of thinking about organizational processes as part of thinking through the recognition of individual autonomy, the encouragement of solidarity, and taking responsibility for the future. How decisions are reached can be as important as the decisions themselves. This is a really important shift, because it moves us away from thinking that organizing is what happens *after* decisions have been taken, and that it can be left to other people. In a society with a complex division of labour, professional politicians and policy makers, global supply chains and gigantic corporations, it is not surprising we should believe this. Most often, the responsibility does not seem to be ours when we swipe a credit card, buy some shoes, or tick a box on a ballot paper. We make a choice, and someone else organizes things for us. But organizing is a decision too, a means and an end, a decision which pre-figures and shapes what follows. Organizing is the solidification of choices, politics made into routines.

In some rather important ways, I also think that these three principles press us to think locally, to think small, because any meaningful use of words like difference, community, sustainability and so on must refer to a particular group of people with names and faces. Otherwise the words are merely hopeful labels with no referent to the times and places where we live our lives. One of the features of the 'there is no alternative' argument is to point to forces outside the local which constrain decision making. 'If it was up to me ...'; 'in an ideal world ...'; 'if we don't do this ...', are all phrases which deny local agency and point to a framework which means that things just have to be like they are. Other people and things – 'competitors', 'the market', 'the student' – can be given the responsibility for the maintenance of the social order. But this buck passing has a cost in terms of the way that it prevents us from thinking that these responsibilities are ours, and that we can imagine different ways that things can be done. That is why many of our alternatives confront us with the local, with what is in front of our noses, because it is there that we spend most of our lives. That being said, small isn't always beautiful, particularly when it comes to the avoidance of insularity and the building of (real and metaphorical) bridges, but it is less likely to do as much damage. In other words, we don't have to assume that organizations must grow and become big corporations, because, in taking our three responsibilities seriously, we might decide that local works better.

Organizations are the result of a particular set of historical, legal and political choices. Accepting that they are not inevitable then opens the possibility of alternatives, but just as important is describing what these other organizational forms might look like. The school for organizing would encourage its students – and employees – to think about organization as a way of making political choices invisible, because they are disguised as means, and hence seem inevitable. But there are lots of other forms of organizing around us already – families, small businesses, local exchange schemes, co-operatives, complementary currencies, intentional communities, voluntary work, barter and so on. Recognizing that all these and more provide different ways of organizing an economy, and that corporate capitalism can hence be put in its place, is the beginning of thinking about organizing as politics.[13]

WE ARE ALL ORGANIZERS

I think that it makes sense to start the teaching at the school for organizing with an encyclopedia of organizing for two reasons. One is that it is empirically accurate. (And accuracy is a helpful place to begin any argument.) The diversity of ways in which human beings have associated with each other, and also combined with all sorts of non-humans, far exceeds any similarities, and only the most committed reductionist would assume otherwise. Of course, humans have organized in order to address some eternal problems – what to eat, who to have sex with, how to create shelter and so on – but the ways in which these problems and others have been solved is creative and multiple. There is no straight line of upward development that takes us from 'then' to 'now', 'there' to 'here', as if the worlds that we live in at the present moment are ones that were the necessary outcome of a historical process, the one best way to be.

My second reason for beginning with variety is political, in the sense that I think that always reminding ourselves that the world is multiple, could be otherwise, does not have to be like this, is a way to ensure that the future is kept open. 'The political', in the way that I understand it, and following the post-structural political theorist Chantal Mouffe,[14] is a word that describes the ceaseless conflict over interests that is characteristic of any human society or form of organization. This is an ontological condition for humans, one that reflects the fact that resources (whether material or cultural) are likely to be limited and hence that there will always be differences of opinion about their distribution and significance. Politics, being a description of meaningful and structured engagements between adversaries, is an inevitable result of the ontological condition of 'the political'. However, it is in the interest of those who currently benefit from any particular social arrangement to persuade others that the present state of affairs is natural, inevitable, the result of a process of evolution or technological change, or a fair distribution based on the capacities or activities of a particular class of people, such as those who are represented within the business school. Well, as we have seen before, they would say that, wouldn't they?

It seems to me that as soon as we accept some version of this account of why the world has to be like it is right now, we foreclose politics. That is why the business school operates as what James Scott calls an 'antipolitics machine', encouraging us to think that we can leave politics on the other side of the rotating door whilst we get on with the business of business. He says that institutions are often antipolitics machines 'designed to turn legitimate political questions into neutral, objective, administrative exercises governed by experts'.[15] This 'depoliticising sleight of hand' results in the naturalization or entrenchment of particular organizational arrangements – a way of placing certain sets of assumptions beyond debate, of suggesting that politics can only apply within certain defined domains (like the voting booth or the council chamber), whilst other decisions have to be left to nature, experts, or kings. In terms of the argument I am making here, it is an attempt to deny the ontology of the political, and hence to move certain matters to being beyond question. Or, as much of the criticism from within the b-school suggests, to be potential objects of mere 'reform', a gentle revision, rather than questioned in any more radical sense.

One of the consequences of contemporary business school education is that it cultivates the idea that only some people can organize. That we need other people, experts, to do the organizing for us because we are too stupid to manage ourselves. But if we ask, 'How are things organized?', we assume very little about what that particular arrangement looks like, or who is in charge, if anyone. Asking about the ways in which human beings arrange and pattern their worlds is a general question, one that might be answered in many different ways. It is a question that certainly might be answered by pointing to management, because that is a form of organization, but it's not the only one. As I said in the previous chapter, the general shape of the question which we are then asking has both a factual and an exploratory element to it: 'How do people and things come together to do stuff?' That's an enquiry which would produce descriptions of the shapes of the worlds that human beings make here and now, and that could be enlarged by adding descriptions from other times and places. The point of collecting such descriptions then also might become a kind of catalogue of possibilities, perhaps answering the question, 'How *can* people and things come together to do stuff?' The catalogue doesn't tell us what we should do, but what we can do, what we are capable of. And when we know that, we can begin to decide what we want to do next.

And that takes me onto the hardest question for this book, because the aim of the school for organizing is to produce graduates who know what human beings are capable of, both good and bad, and who want to use that knowledge to engage in reflexive organization. But why should students want to come to the school for organizing, when the business school keeps promising so much?

9

What do students want?

It's easy to criticize the students who attend the business school, suggesting perhaps that it is an institution which attracts people who are selfish and seduced by the glamour of power and wealth. Greedy pigs in power suits. Or perhaps that it makes people like that, because it teaches selfishness and the glamour of power and wealth. They spend so long snuffling at the trough that their snouts start to grow. There are comparative moral judgements here, as if the student who studies physics or the history of art is somehow doing it for more noble reasons than the one who chooses a business degree. I don't want to engage in that sort of finger pointing, because of the cultural elitism that it trades on, but also because it doesn't seem like a very helpful way of moving forward. I need the students on my side, not pushed into a position in which they have to defend themselves and point the finger back at me. So this chapter will make the case for why students should want to study at the school for organizing, rather than at the b-school. I will make this case with a combination of arguments relating to the idea of a university, the regulation of professional training, and the importance of university marketing departments in moving away from selling greed and sloganizing about ambition, to instead focusing on sustainable, diverse and responsible business courses. In summary, I will suggest that prospective and actual students currently have their views of organizing shaped by higher education, so the question is not whether they can be shaped differently, because they can, but how.

PUBLIC AND PRIVATE GOODS

Most of this book contains a pretty simple argument, one that is quite easy to make. You might not agree with it, but the logic is clear enough. In the last few years, I have been presenting various versions of the argument in a variety of places and I'm getting pretty good at dealing with the sort of questions I get. Indeed, I bat the questions away with some enthusiasm, demonstrating the absolute clarity of my position and the inexorable logic that leads me there. But the question I continue to worry about is the one about students. You see, the problem is that students keep on turning up at the revolving door of the business school in increasing numbers, in all sorts of different universities and in all parts of the world. If the institution were as myopic, corrupted and vacuous as I have suggested, they wouldn't keep turning up, would they? Or I am I just saying that they are all stupid, brain-washed idiots who deserve what they get?

It's a tricky thing to call all those people stupid, particularly the young and impressionable undergraduates, fresh of face and ready for learning. I don't mind insulting the older students, and I certainly don't mind insulting my colleagues, or the people who run and fund higher education, but to blame 18-year-olds for the dreadful state of the business school does seem a bit like blaming babies for the taste of baby food. It's just not their fault.

In order to understand how to deal with the question, we have to begin with some ideas about education and what it is for. Summarizing very quickly, we could suggest that either education is a 'public good' – something that benefits the majority in a given society – or a 'private good' – something that an individual benefits from. In economics, this distinction is a helpful way to distinguish between a park and a cheeseburger, but a moment's thought shows that there are lots of 'goods' that don't fit easily into that tidy binary opposition. Endless debates about the ownership and control of transport, utilities, or health care in different countries would serve to illustrate the moving line between public and private here. It's not a simple matter, particularly when it comes to the education and training of people and the sort of 'good' (in both senses of the term) which that provides for others and themselves. Educating the young is more often seen to be a public good, but the education of adults can be understood as something that can be categorized as a private good, perhaps because of the financial and personal satisfactions that it can provide. However, certain occupations are often deemed to be more public than others in this regard. So, if we agree that we need doctors, and that therefore we should train doctors, then it is often the state which will pay for that training. And what about engineers, social workers, schoolteachers, dentists, nurses, pharmacists, clinical psychologists, perhaps even architects? All these are occupations that, many would argue, have a strong claim to be understood as doing something that benefits everyone, and hence that the costs of training should be met, at least in part, by the public purse. The same argument can easily enough be extended to cover 'pure' subjects in science and medicine that are regarded to be essential to technical progress – chemistry, biology and physics, geology, information technology and medical research.

So far, so good, but what happens with forms of education that don't lead so directly into valued occupations, or that aren't so clearly tied to ideas about scientific and technical progress? This basically covers the general mush of the social sciences, arts and humanities. It is not so easy to argue that sociology, geography, or cultural studies are essential to the running of a complex society, or are vital elements in technological development. Indeed, in order to make that argument, you need to accept some broader ideas about the role that education plays in a society. These are necessarily vague, but might stress the importance of the best that has been thought and said in arts and literature in cultivating and civilizing citizens, the idea that the study of history, place and space are part of human self-understanding, or that studying politics, media and communication is one way to ensure an open society. Back to the idea of the university again then.

In terms of the distinction between public and private goods, it seems that it rather depends on where we start. A relentless pro-market private goods position is likely to begin with, for example, art history, and ask just why the public should be paying for someone to study something so elitist, and argue that – since graduates tend to have higher salaries than non-graduates – they can pay for the costs of this course themselves. Studying art history is then placed in the same category as buying a piece of art for your home, or deciding to eat at an expensive restaurant. It's a luxury that you will benefit from, and you should pay for it yourself. The logic of this starting position can then roll through the humanities and social sciences, marketizing the university as it goes. But if we start with the training of nurses, then it becomes easier to argue that all higher education is a public good, because it contributes to the sum total of skill and wisdom within any society. Graduates perform many different social roles and occupations, and their value cannot be restricted to some rather than others – as if health care mattered more than museums, or schoolteachers trump film-makers.

Enter the business school, stage right. As I have already suggested, the b-school (in many parts of the world) has been a very clear case of the private goods argument. It has sold itself on its usefulness for individuals, shouting about salary increases, the opportunity to work in exciting places, jump on aeroplanes a lot, and do important things for which you will be admired. The appeal has been to 'make the most of yourself', to become the sort of person who gets jobs with global blue-chip corporations, to be a 'leader'. These are not appeals to the collective, to the social, but to the student who means business, who wants a job that pays well and allows them to live in London, New York, or

Tokyo, striding purposefully with a well-tooled briefcase into a mirrored skyscraper. Business schools have made it difficult to see their products as public goods, since they relentlessly market self-interest, shouting loudly at passing customers.

STUDENTS AND CUSTOMERS

Now, setting aside the wider questions about the funding of students, consider what the appeal to the private goods argument does to ideas about education. Bear in mind that the student has been sold a course based on the idea that it will benefit them directly, in terms of their skill development, employability, starting salary, leadership qualities, entrepreneurial spirit, or whatever. No wonder then that they might imagine themselves as customers, or that the business school itself might treat them as customers. The customer is someone who engages in a transaction, and who is perfectly entitled to complain if the supplier failed to provide what was advertised. If the cheeseburger has no cheese, I expect it to be replaced, or I want my money back. If the meal in the expensive restaurant was a cheeseburger, I would probably want my money back too, unless it was made from some super-expensive Japanese beef that had been massaged with sake and sung lullabies when the moon came up.

Now it follows from this description of the supplier-customer relationship that the job of the supplier/b-school is to find out what students want and provide it to them. As we saw in Chapter 5, market research, advertising and branding, product design and innovation, staff recruitment, even architecture, become driven by ideas about student choice, satisfaction and recommendation. There are sometimes various proxies in this relationship, as there are in other consumer-supplier relationships. Just as a consumer organization might provide rankings of electrical items or insurance products, so do state agencies, newspapers and magazines, knowledge corporations and professional associations provide rankings and kitemarks for business schools. Being 'triple accredited', or occupying an elevated place in a league table, is one of the ways in which students gather the information to make choices, so developing strategies which focus on the data that goes into league tables is a rational response. The tables produced by newspapers owned by media companies such as *Business Week* (which started to publish b-school tables in 1988), the *Financial Times* (1999), the *Wall Street Journal* (2001) and *The Economist* (2002), become very important in determining the branding and sales strategy of the school.[1] Whether it is the number of staff with PhDs, the starting salary of graduates, or the make-up of an external advisory board, the measure becomes the focus of management intervention within the school. And league tables can feed other league tables, as they do in terms of the way that b-school rankings are partly parasitic on state rankings of research, which in turn are shaped by various rankings of the world's best academic journals to publish in. This is a tangled nest of hierarchies and ratings, one that produces a hyper-sensitivity to proxy customers, like a teenager who preens in the mirror, and worries incessantly about how they are seen by others.

But this is not madness. Indeed, it is entirely logical, once the opinions of the customer are assumed to be dominant, which follows from the idea that what the business school sells is a private good. The school for organizing is doomed before it has even begun, in such circumstances. How will the school for organizing wheedle and lie its way up the rankings? Who would launch a product that so few people wanted to buy? Where is the market research for all this?

INFORMATION ASYMMETRY

One of the many problems that bedevils those who are keen on market-based ideas of exchange is the problem of how customers get knowledge about what they are buying. This isn't so much of a difficulty when the product is cheap, replaceable and its utility is easily established. If it's a burger, you can taste it, spit it out and ask for something else instead. If it's more expensive, harder to substitute and its utility can only be established over a long period of use – a car, for example – then the balance of power starts to shift to the suppliers, because they can say all sorts of things about their product that aren't necessarily true, and the consumer has less information to go on, as well as judgements that might take years to make. No wonder lots of consumers use league tables, star charts, and recommendations as a way of making decisions. It's just a way of levelling the playing field.

But what if the product being sold is knowledge? What if the consumer is purchasing expertise? The relationship between a student and the university can't only be described in terms of buyers and sellers for precisely this reason. The student doesn't know what they need to know, and they have to trust that the teacher, the researcher, the academic does know more than they do. Information asymmetry is built into the exchange, and this gives it rather a different character.

If we were to suggest, for example, that the student should be able to determine the curriculum, this would already suggest that they knew what they needed to know, and hence had no need for the exchange in the first place. This isn't an argument for being authoritarian, for claiming that the professional always knows best, but a statement about the necessary relationship between teachers and students in conventional universities.[2] If we go back to where we started, with the example of doctors, it would be unlikely that even the most radical critic of education would propose that students already know about the medical science of the human body before they go to medical school. Students go to universities to find out how to make bridges that don't fall down, or laptop computers that do whatever it is that my laptop is doing now, or discover what human beings know about the structure of atoms and stars. Students don't know these things, before they go there, which is why they go there.

This means that many characteristics of the relationship that a student has with their university, or a student has with their teacher, are not at all like that of a consumer. It is reasonable to expect that academics in a particular field should be able to have considerable influence over the sort of things that students study, the ways in which they learn about them and the means by which they are assessed for their competence in those fields. If these minimal preconditions are not met, then there is very little justification for the university at all. *Enl*

So, if we can't simply treat students as consumers, how does that corrode the idea of education as a private good?

SOCIAL GOODS

One of the blindingly obvious things to say about the university, about any form of education, is that it changes people. Not always to the same degree, and not always in predictable ways, but it does change people. So since there are lots of universities, and lots of students, the impact of universities on the societies of which they are a part is collectively considerable. They are institutions which cultivate and transmit beliefs and behaviours, both through their explicit and hidden curricula. The ideas that these institutions incubate play a part in shaping the world we live in, as well as the ways in which we understand the constraints of the past and the possibilities of the future.

Of course, we might say this about lots of different institutions that have an influence on the world – companies that sell mobile phones, manufacture alcohol, make cars – but in all of those cases it would also be widely agreed that there should be regulations about using mobile phones while driving cars, selling alcohol to young people, and driving cars too fast. We collectively agree that we have an interest in regulating certain forms of production and consumption. In fact, we do this all the time. As I suggested earlier in the book, markets are rarely completely free and unconstrained, but are always regulated by state agencies and the force of law, as well as by ethical and political conventions. Consider the sale of body parts, guns, literature that denies the Holocaust, pornography, drugs, slave labour, children and so on. Regulating markets, or exchange relationships more generally, is not a problem, and we do it all the time.

So, if we have an institution which changes people, and agree that regulating markets is a rule rather than an exception, then there is no objection in principal to the idea of intervening in business education. In other words, we could assume that there is a collective interest at stake here. Since the ideas that business schools sell will contribute to shaping all our futures, then they should be subject to wider debate. The only way that business schools can escape that demand is by claiming that what they do has no consequence, no effects on the world, but since they are always noisily claiming the opposite, then they should expect the reciprocal demands for accountability.

To make this argument is to suggest that the b-school qualification should not be treated as a private good. Perhaps it's not quite a public good either, in the same sense as a road or a park, but it is something that has effects on others. Let's call this a 'social' good, to point to the idea that the production and consumption of this good has effects that aren't simply private.[3] That is another reason why the idea that 'the customer is king' is a problem when it comes to university education. Students are not in a position to claim expertise over the knowledge that they wish to purchase, but this knowledge is also having effects on others because it will – to a greater or lesser degree – shape the way that they behave after they have graduated.

All that I am trying to do here is to establish the idea that leaving business education to 'the market' is actually a political choice, just as intervening in it in the way that I suggest is a political choice. Political choices should not be foreclosed, with an assertion about 'the market' being used to feed the antipolitics machine. So a thoughtful answer to the question I set for this chapter 'What do students want?', actually means questioning whether students really do know what they want (because of the information problem) and whether students are the only ones who should be asked to respond to this question (because of the social consequences of business school education). So, let me ask the question slightly differently, who wants the school for organizing?

WHO WANTS CHANGE?

This book has argued that the sort of world that is being produced by the market managerialism that the business school sells is not a pleasant one. It's a sort of utopia for the wealthy and powerful, a group that the students are encouraged to imagine themselves joining, but such privilege is brought at a very high cost, resulting in environmental catastrophe, resource wars and forced migration, inequality within and between countries, the encouragement of hyper-consumption as well as persistently anti-democratic practices in work organizations.

Selling the business school works by ignoring these problems, or by mentioning them as challenges and then ignoring them in the practices of teaching and research. As we have seen, there might be modules on Business Ethics or Sustainability or Diversity or Corporate Social Responsibility, but these are add-ons, not the core elements of a business course. I am suggesting that the idea that there might be many different ways of doing business, of arranging an economy, of imagining forms of organization, needs to be built into the school in a much more fundamental way than this. But who is likely to want to encourage such a change?

There seem to me to be four potential groups with interests here, and they are not mutually exclusive, though each has different obstacles and potentials. One is to rely on the state or state agencies to regulate higher education markets or encourage business schools to move in the direction of the school for organizing. This is the least likely option, simply because it requires that politicians and policy makers see votes in intervening in business school education, and that seems rather unlikely at present, particularly because the b-school has been the cash machine that has provided a lot of the money that allowed governments to drive down higher education funding. Radical change to the business school sounds like killing the goose that lays such a big golden egg, so let's agree that change from that quarter is unlikely.

The second, which is just as unlikely, is that professional associations and other interest groups push business schools to fully integrate alternatives into their teaching and research. And, because I can hear the outraged cries already, I don't mean option modules, but a sustained, loud and insistent attempt to entirely reconfigure the curriculum. The problem is that for most professional associations, such as those representing different national collections of business school academics, or MBA students, or specialisms like accounting or operations management, or European business schools, or business school deans (and yes, all of those exist), there is nothing particularly broken about the status quo and hence nothing that really needs fixing. There will be periodic attempts to mumble about the importance of the environment, or to hand-wring about the 'bottom of the pyramid', or to wonder whether stratospheric pay inequalities are justifiable, but for all of these organizations their core business relies on having lots of business schools, lots of b-school academics and lots of business students, so I suggest rocking of the boat isn't likely to come from this quarter either.

That's not completely true, because there are some organizations that are trying to intervene in more productive ways – the most notable of these being the United Nations initiative on the Principle for Responsible Management Education (PRME). This is an initiative that began in 2006, growing out of the UN's 'Global Compact', a framework for businesses which sets aspirations in ten areas – human rights, labour, the environment and so on. Under the coordination of the UN Global Compact and (at the time of writing), 673 business schools, the PRME task force has developed a set of six principles which lay the foundation for a global understanding of what it might mean to be 'responsible' in management education. It's a noble initiative, one that is trying to inspire and lobby for a very desirable direction of change. The problem is that, despite the large number of signatories and the moral weight of the UN, it has no leverage in terms of actually changing what business schools do. Principal two of the six, for example, says that 'We will incorporate into our academic activities and curricula the values of global social responsibility as portrayed in international initiatives such as the United Nations Global Compact.'[4] This is entirely aspirational, as well as being endearingly vague. It's nice to have the PRME kitemark on your website, but the kitemark is easy to get and hard to lose. There is also no evidence that students are particularly interested in whether a b-school has the kitemark or not, as opposed to one of the other big three accreditations, which clearly do matter in marketing terms. Sadly, the PRME has no muscle.

A third group that we might look to with more optimism are the academics themselves, the staff who actually work within the b-schools. Indeed, this book has grown from the experience of one of those people, a migrant from sociology who found himself in a strange land that made him uneasy, and this is the latest version of my response. The collective experience of those who claim some sort of general identification with Critical Management Studies is the context for this work, and it's those people who are the choir to whom I am very often preaching. It would seem obvious that if the majority of the academics who administrate, teach and research within business schools are convinced by the argument I make here, then things will change. Of course it requires a sort of paradigm shift in the way that 'organizing' is understood, but then such changes in fashion and core theory are built into the idea of scientific progress, so there is no intrinsic reason why academic staff themselves couldn't press for changes to the curriculum, different research programmes, different textbooks and so on. The problem is that there is very little evidence of that actually happening.

Critical Management Studies is a small and largely invisible part of the average business school in a few countries of the Global North. I'd love to think that the academics were going to ride to the rescue, but I just don't think that it's the case. It has some noisy voices, a few conferences and journals, but next to no influence over the formulation of policy and strategy for virtually all business schools. Indeed, in most of the really prestigious b-schools, particularly the US ones, it might as well not exist at all. So even if CMS academics, combined with sympathetic academics from other areas, did engage in some sort of heroic struggle for the dark heart of the business school, it's pretty unlikely that they would be noticed, let alone have some sort of effect. Bear in mind that CMS academics, as well as many others, have been aiming their barbs at the b-school for years now, and when the beast notices them, it actually rewards them for getting published in good journals. To make matters worse, many CMS sympathizers are far too busy debating the usual range of topics in epistemology and methods, as well as themselves benefiting from the present set-up. I, like many of my colleagues, have a comfortable and well-paid job, frequent trips to conferences in nice parts of the world, as well as a mortgage to pay, children's university fees to fund and holidays to take. What's not to like?

It seems to me that most of the likely suspects – the state, the associations, the academics – simply benefit too much from the way that things are to be the vanguards of any revolution, so let's not look there. I suppose things might change when the first business school sinks beneath the rising waves,[5] but (attractive though the idea of a business school full of fish might be) for now let's assume I'm not going to get a great deal of help from that quarter. Instead, I want to concentrate on the group that present the biggest obstacle and the biggest opportunity: the students themselves.

SELLING THE FUTURE

It isn't really surprising that we come back to students at the end of this chapter, because they are the beginning and the end of the university, of education itself. In that, the marketizers are correct. Students shouldn't be taken for granted, and their voices should be listened to, and their assignments marked in a reasonable period of time and with generous and thought-provoking feedback. But, as I have argued already, students aren't customers. What they appear to want isn't always right simply because they appear to say that they want it. Just because someone chooses to eat fast food all the time doesn't mean that they are informed about, or have access to, or can afford, healthy fresh food. If there are no alternatives, then there is no choice. The same is true of students. They aren't exercising informed choice, balancing this against that, largely because they aren't actually being offered any choice at all. In fact, they are being told that there are no choices, and that this is what an education in business and management should like, because it can't look like anything else. There isn't anything else to have.

And this is because, despite all their needy claims to distinctiveness and relevance, most business schools most of the time just want to be like every other business school. Like penguins huddling against the cold, they push themselves towards the warm middle, the centre of the huddle, fearing being on the outside, alone. It's pretty odd really, since the Marketing 101 course that they teach in one of the packed lecture theatres would tell them that imitation is only one market strategy, and in a crowded market (one filled with squawking penguins who all look and sound like each other) it might even make sense to be different. To offer something that all the other places don't offer (perhaps a business school full of fish.)

Offering choice is exactly what I propose here, and it's an irony that it's an argument that I want to make in a context in which choice appears to be all around. Different institutions, different degrees, different modules, different modes of study – but most of them exactly the same, a recitation of the inevitability of one way of arranging the world, and adding up to a chorus that tells the student that nothing significant can ever change. It's the hidden curriculum again then, in two senses. The first is the meaning I was using in Chapter 2, of something hiding in the light, something too obvious to say. The jabbering consensus is that this is the only way that the world can work, because this is how people and markets and organizations are, and it doesn't need saying because it is all around us, in the careers talks and sponsored lecture theatres and the best-selling textbooks. The other way of thinking about the hidden curriculum is the opposite, a deafening silence, to an absence in which alternatives are hidden from sight, or placed in a few dusty boxes for curios, failed experiments and nostalgia. Who, apart from the weirdos, would want to go and look there?

If you want to make someone want something, you have to start by telling them that it exists, and that is exactly what the school for organizing will be doing. But you also have to give them a reason to make the choice you want them to make. So let me say some obvious things.

The young people who are considering studying business in the Global North know that the business school is a tarnished institution and that businesspeople are considered by many to be crooks or dullards. As we saw earlier, they have grown up in a culture that tells them just that through *The Simpsons* and Hollywood films, and that gives them a clear sense that many people don't trust business and that being successful at work involves behaving like a competitor on *The Apprentice* who would sell his grandmother for a chance at the job, or being a Trumpish idiot pointing his stubby finger and shouting. When they tell people that they are studying business or management, the reactions that they get are probably enough to tell them what many people think about what they are doing.

The young people who are considering studying in business schools also know a few other things. They also know that the Earth is warming fast, and that bankers' salaries are telephone numbers whilst in some other quarters of the world dead-eyed children starve in their mothers' arms. They know that people sleep in the doorways of the shops in their cities, and that sometimes you can taste the chemicals in the air, which means that you often wear a mask. They know that adverts lie and marketing is a glossy sham, and that animal species are becoming extinct at an accelerating rate. They know that the sea is full of plastic, people in sweatshops in Bangladesh make cheap clothes for them, and that a McDonald's double cheese and fries diet is bad for you. They also know that businesses try to avoid paying taxes, and regularly conceal problems with their products. None of this is new to the students. None of this shocks them.

It really isn't as if the people who enter business school need to have the scales lifted from their eyes. They might need to be reminded of some things, but they aren't idiots. What they don't have, or many of them don't have, is a sense that the world could be organized differently. They are simply confronted with the massive edifice of the way that things are, which they know is a bit shit, and are told that it's not their fault that the world is like this, which it isn't. It just is what it is – get used to it. Any colour you like as long as its globalizing consumer capitalism, because there isn't any other colour available. Or, as Frederic Jameson said, or rather he said that someone else said, 'it is easier to imagine the end of the world than to imagine the end of capitalism.'[6]

(And oddly, at the same time, we are in a golden age for sci-fi and fantasy, in which escapist and subversive imaginings of other worlds, other ways of being together and being human are ubiquitous in films, comic books, video games and cosplay conventions. Metrosexual pirates, courageous space farers, outlaws and brave hobbits challenge the established order of things, demand justice, and very often win through against the dark forces in the tower.[7])

The number of times b-schools refer to choice and voice is inverse proportion to the actual choices and voices that they offer. Not only is this a political problem, in terms of the way that it limits the horizons of possibility and places matters of business and economy outside politics, it also ends up producing a fraudulent half-discipline which presents its truths as if they were the only truths. So students know that there are problems, but they have little faith in the potential of the business school or any other institution to solve them. They are stuck in what Peter Benson and Stuart Kirsch call the 'politics of resignation', an ironic distance from the way that the world works, but having no sense of any mechanisms that might be used to change it. I'm not sure that students need to be taught 'critical thinking skills' as such. I think they need to be convinced that the application of those skills could make a difference to the world that they live in, to 'unlock the folded arms of cynicism'.[8] The school for organizing is some kind of answer. Why not tell students this?

There is no need to hide the school for organizing, no need to camouflage it as a kinder b-school – just tell and sell it like it is. Explain to prospective students that they can study a subject that takes the horrors of the world seriously, and offers to do something about them. Sell them a vision of a future which is not a Groundhog Day version of the present, which shows them other places and times, and offers them a place in making sure that the world that they will play a part in making will be better than that which we inhabit at the present time. This means being as loudly enthusiastic as conventional business schools, with the advantage that what is being sold is a social good, as well as being a subject that takes all forms of organizing seriously.

There are a lot of awful clichés about the optimism of youth and the pessimism of age, if the young only could and if the old only would, but they have some truth that can be traded in this context. The sad thing about the business school is that it is a device for crushing possibility, an antipolitics machine, or to be more precise, for reducing the possible to a straight and narrow path. The young people, and the older ones too, are made old before their time, made into realists. But if the young aren't going to be idealists, then who is, and if the university isn't going to encourage imaginative exploration, then where is?

There is a gamble here of course, because no one can guarantee that the school for organizing will slide easily into the world. There are many forces arranged against it – the state and policy makers, professional associations, even academics themselves – all of whom benefit in various ways from the present order. That means that the school for organizing is likely to have to persuade students to want to study there if it is to be a viable project. That's just fine, because it should be easy to persuade the very people who have the most direct stake in the world that they are going to make and live in. The US inventor Charles Kettering, Head of Research at General Motors for many years, once said 'I'm interested in the future because I'm going to spend the rest of my life there.'[9] His imagined future was a 1930s one of cheap gas and lots of cars. That's not the sort of future that my students will live in, but they still do have an interest in the future. They just need reminding of that.

IO

The business school of tomorrow[1]

> Since we can speak of what transcends the language of the
> present only in the language of the present we risk cancelling
> our imaginings in the very act of articulating them. The only
> real otherness would be that which we could not articulate
> at all.
>
> Terry Eagleton[2]

If we did think that we were the cleverest people who had
ever lived (or at least were effectively working for people who
seemed to think that of themselves), we might believe that we
have already found the best way to organize, and that the words
that are currently used to describe this form of organization
(management, business, commerce) should become synonyms
for organization. (Which would be a bit like saying that all plants
are ivy.) The fact that the people who are fond of 'management'
ideas are also powerful, and can provide universities with chairs,
corporate art, and glass atriums, undoubtedly helps academics
with their amnesia about other organizational forms. It is easier
if business schools forget that they are schooling people to
reproduce market managerialism, and to dismiss all these other
organizings to other departments, other times, other places, other
people's problems. We can only see the ivy from our windows,
and so all plants must be ivy. They are not:

> The plant world exhibits astonishing diversity. Plants vary from
> microscopic, one celled algae to huge trees such as the Giant

Redwoods of California, towering some 300 feet or more into the sky. In between these two extremes is a bewildering array of more than a quarter of a million naturally occurring species and uncounted numbers of cultivars developed by man during more than 2000 years of cultivation and selection.[3]

Would you study somewhere that only taught you about one plant? Would you listen to a gardener who appeared to believe that plants from other places and other times were irrelevant to the obsessive cultivation of this one species? Who regarded everything else as weeds, a mess that needed to be tidied and made to stand in line by the wise and well trained?[4]

I began the first chapter of this book by walking you into an imaginary business school. It was an antiseptic place. Scandinavian airport architecture, a murmur of laptops and an air of self-importance. Now, assuming that the good fairy grants me all my wishes, that decision makers read this book, policy makers decide to fund and regulate university education, taxpayers agree, funders pay up and students turn up, what would it be like walking into the school for organizing? I think there are two answers to that question, futures one and two. I'll start with the less radical one, the easy one.

THE UNIVERSITY SCHOOL FOR ORGANIZING

In future one, you are again in a university, somewhere near somewhere in the Global North. The business school building is now used by some other department, or perhaps occupied noisily for childcare, and the new school has been set up in a social sciences or humanities building, a building which is not sponsored by a corporation or well-trousered magnate.[5] The parking is difficult, and the flower beds are unkempt. Inside, the place looks untidy, with posters hanging off noticeboards by a single pin, hairy students obstructing corridors with their feet, and confused and confusing academics with bad haircuts running around being late for things. It looks, in other words, pretty much like the rest of the university.[6] This school for organizing researches and teaches everything from Angelic Choirs to the Zapatistas, and does not restrict itself to inter-breeding varieties of market managerialism. This will be a place where students want to study because it teaches about interesting things, and hopefully teaches about them in interesting ways.[7] This will be a school for people who want to learn from other places, other times, other politics, and to consider the relevance of these lessons for their own attempts to create and participate in organizations. The school will try to work with governments and big businesses, because they matter, but it will spend a lot more energy trying to ensure that it engages with small businesses, alternatives and experiments, marginalized communities, NGOs, charities and community groups in its local area. This doorway to knowledge will need to be kept open for everyone, not just those who have a sense of entitlement or a great deal of cash.

All the usual academic business school disciplines are still being taught here – accounting, marketing, operations and so on – but their context and aims are no longer assumed, because they are being applied to different problems. Accounting is no longer about finding and hiding profits; marketing works for the people who buy things, not just the people who sell them; and operations now values carbon emissions more highly than speed or price. Capitalism, and its management, are taught as one arrangement amongst many others, and not presumed to be as ubiquitous and inevitable as oxygen. This means that the business disciplines or functions are applied to settings which question their standard assumptions, and as a result they are made more expansive by being tested against a wide variety of forms of organizing. The students are studying courses in 'Finance and co-operatives 101', an elective on 'The marketing of non-profits', a third-year core course on 'Localizing, degrowth and the economy'; and an option taught by the philosophy department called 'Freedom and slavery at work'. Other options cover:

> Roman military organization; book-keeping and the role of the monastery in medieval times; the management of the artist's workshop in the Renaissance; the interaction of research funding (from wealthy patrons) and artistic excellence; the formation and mechanization of manufacturing in the nineteenth century; the birth of marketing and public relations ...[8]

As long as the concern is organizing – how people and things come together to do stuff – then there are no restrictions on when, where and what is or was being organized. If we think of organizing as a form of socio-technical design, a conscious patterned arrangement of people and things, then inspiration might come from all sorts of sources – artistic, interdisciplinarity, historical and so on.[9] A good designer will feed their ideas by going to art galleries, museums and films, because if you are not merely reproducing that which exists now, then you never know where the next idea might come from.

It might be said that I am simply including too much here, shoehorning everything into organizing, making an imperial claim for a particular term and then subordinating everything to it. What isn't organizing? Is the net simply being spread too widely? I think that is probably true, but then I do want the school for organizing to be porous and inclusive, both in terms of objects of enquiry, but also methods and epistemologies. I'm not sure that this is so much of a problem though. Just as physicists like to claim that everything is physics, or psychologists insist on the centrality of the human mind, economics concerns itself with aggregations of interests, or geographers see all phenomena as concerned with space and place, so does the school for organizing claim a certain sort of centrality to understanding the ways that human beings come together to co-ordinate. Other disciplines will contest, or contextualize, this claim, debating the dotted lines which separate this discipline from that one. It doesn't really matter though, because at least the school for organizing (unlike the b-school) will be beginning with a concept, rather than a statement of affiliation.

The school for organizing is a laboratory in which the future is being built.[10] It will provide imaginative resources for its students to do their own organizing, as well as requiring them to consider the ways in which any form of organizing produces particular sorts of freedoms, communities and futures. We could call this 'reflexive organizing', or 'meta-organizing', in the sense that it is a politics machine, demanding that its students see words like 'efficiency', 'profits', 'leadership' and all the rest as contestable claims, not statements of fact. This is an attempt to disclose politics, rather than foreclosing it. Bear in mind Plato's concern with the education of his guardians in *The Republic*. In order to secure the future for all citizens, the guardians need to be trained to be thoughtful, modest, compassionate – to not be tyrants who think that they know everything. This is education which intentionally opens the possibility that there are many, many other shapes and shades in which organization might happen. Now, in order to remind you of this fact, because it is a fact, let me take one more example of an organization that seems to be breaking many rules, but has been thriving for nearly two decades.

PREMIUM-COLA

Premium-Cola[11] is an Internet collective that grew from the hacker culture around Hamburg, Germany, and which began organizing the manufacturing and distribution of a highly caffeinated cola drink in 2001. They have no office, no fixed salaries, and no formal boss – just a moderator who looks after the discussion board. Premium-Cola is only sold in outlets in Germany whose ethos is similar to that of the brand, and they never export outside Germany because of the carbon costs associated with moving the product. Around 1,700 partners participate, some more intensively than others, and anyone – whether supplier, distributor, or customer – is positively encouraged to take part in decision making. For some members, Premium is a hobby, for others it is a full-time job. Most importantly, all issues are decided on collectively, and with high levels of discussion and expectations of trust. There are no written contracts, just a general assumption that all decisions must be fair to all the members of the network. This means that they do not aim at growth for its own sake, or at maximizing profits by squeezing any other members of the collective.

Premium considers itself an 'open-source economy' organization, and is entirely transparent about what it calls its continually revised 'operating system' in order to encourage other businesses to use their model. The Premium Collective want to show how it is possible to have a business that assumes equal rights, equal pay, and consensus democratic decision making on every topic that the members regard to be important to discuss. There are no shareholders, no managers who earn more than everyone else, and all the money circulating in the network goes back into the system to ensure fair pay for everyone, including the growers of raw materials, manufacturers, distributors and customers. They aim to produce a fully transparent organization, with even their bank account being open for all members of the collective to see.

Consider a few examples of how this works in practice. Premium have been approached by quite a few companies across Europe who wish to sell their products, or to manufacture them under some sort of franchise agreement. After discussions, the collective decided that they didn't want to enter into these sorts of arrangements. The carbon costs of exporting outside Germany were simply too high, and they had no interest in being responsible for a franchisee. In any case, they had imagined themselves as an 'open-source' company, so they simply suggested to the enquirers that they could make the drink themselves, as long as they didn't export their product into Germany. Premium would supply them with the recipe, as well as all the information about the way that the company organizes its business. At the time of writing, Premium are working with a Danish company in order to help them do exactly this.

Or, think about the following. Premium use a variety of distributors, and they were approached by one of their larger ones asking for a volume discount. This is not uncommon after all, with purchasers who have substantial buying power and wish to use that to gain some advantage in market terms. Again, this issue was discussed online by the collective. They decided that they didn't see why an organization which was already making a lot of money from moving Premium products should be enabled to make even more, so weren't happy with that idea. However, they were aware of the danger of being overly reliant on a few large distributors, and keen to diversify the range of distributors that they used. As a result, they decided to incentivize smaller distributors by offering them an 'anti-volume discount'. Now, the smaller distributors pay less for the product than the bigger ones.

Both of these examples might seem counter-intuitive to anyone who assumes that a business, with its demands for growth and market share, would always act in order to maximize its profits. Particularly a business that manufactures fizzy sugar water, because this isn't a company that makes locally sourced lentil-based snacks. In this case, however, the relentless logic of an organization that wants to be fair, tries to make every decision democratically, and to ensure that everyone involved with the organization – cocoa growers, hacker customers who want to stay up all night, people who work in a bottling plant, lorry drivers, bar owners – has a say, means that the decisions are not those that might be expected. Or rather, are not those that might be expected if we assume that all organizations are like corporations, and that everyone just wants to reproduce capitalism. The partly virtual nature of Premium might also be of interest, since many authors have been suggesting that the rise of social media and network technologies produces very different possibilities for organizing, contractions of time and space that make the time-consuming process of institution building unnecessary.[12] So of course, Premium-Cola will be invited to talk to the students at the school for organizing, and perhaps their insights and expertise in running a collective might inspire others to try and do something similar. That way, another future will be invented.

DESCHOOLING ORGANIZING

> A spider conducts operations that resemble those of a weaver, and a bee puts to shame many an architect in the construction of her cells. But what distinguishes the worst architect from the best of bees is this, that the architect raises his structure in imagination before he erects it in reality.
>
> Karl Marx, *Capital: Volume 1*

In a sense, Marx was right, of course. Architects and bees are different. But embedded within this insight about the capacities of human beings to plan and pattern their world is another assumption, that people need other people to plan for them. I suppose we might expect that from Marx. He was a Marxist after all, and many of his disciples have assumed that a strong leader and party discipline is the only way to get things done. Just like the building in your local university with a grand sign that proclaims the 'University of X Department of Management', or 'The [insert rich man's name here] Business School'. Within that building, people are teaching ideas about management, a practice conducted by leaders and their many minions. Meanwhile, in the rest of the world, a great deal of organizing is going on – in places like Suma, Premium and all the many other organizations that have decided to question the common sense of the business school. Bees too, in hives and human imitations of hives, in swarms and multitudes, seem to cope without advice from b-schools.

The performative problem for the school for organizing is just how it avoids becoming just another concentration of expertise, another collection of people telling other people just what they should do, including how to read Marx. In 1971, the anarchist philosopher and activist Ivan Illich published a book called *Deschooling Society*.[13] He argues that schools have become places that hoard knowledge and then funnel it in order to control and reward those who have conformed to certain expectations. The university, he suggests, has become a recruiting centre for companies, a training ground for consumption and a justification for the disposal of those who cannot be 'schooled'. Instead, he suggests, schooling needs to be re-imagined as more a web of communication, in which people learn from each other without the certificates, the bending of the knee, the training in obedience. His programme is to disestablish schooling, and invent learning as a relationship between people.

This is the second future for the school for organizing, not a cosy life as a new department of a university, snuggled in next to sociology and politics and with a good pension, but an insistence that we are all organizers. Perhaps the school for organizing needs to be outside the university, or at least at arms' length distance from it. It needs to be open to all who need to learn about organizing, and perhaps this throws us back to that pre-industrial sense of 'managery' as a kind of coping, a way of dealing with the complexities and contradictions of life. Remember that it was not a particular skill which could be codified outside particular circumstances, not a practice engaged in by a special cadre of people who get paid more because they have a particular kind of knowledge. Managing is something we all do, some better and some worse, but we are all engaged in it, one way or another. So in this future, schooling is dispersed, because the alternative to the business school is not a new school, but no school at all. Instead, we have networks of different densities and concentrations, organizations of the organizationless,[14] people doing whatever it was that they did before the business school was even a glimmer in a Frenchman's eye.

As with most either/or choices, futures one and two both have their attractions and their problems. The first is held in place by the idea of the university, probably by public funding secured through another big organization that deserves our suspicion: the state. The university school for organizing trades on ideas about professional experts being visited by supplicants, and gives qualifications in return for jumping through hoops. Future two requires an exodus from the universities. It deschools knowledge about how to organize, insists that this is a general capacity for human beings, but tells us nothing, in advance, concerning what sort of things might be learned, by who, or to what end.

For myself, I think that the school for organizing would be ill-advised to give up on the idea of the university, but that it should always be haunted by its outside, and never forget that managery surrounds it. This is partly what Stefano Harney and Fred Moten seem to be proposing with their idea that the university can be subverted through the occupation of its 'undercommons', the exploitation of the spaces and resources that it provides in order to provide opportunities for 'study', not schooling.[15] Harney and Moten remind us that institutions are dangerous things, because they harden and fix, but nonetheless that they always have gaps which can be inhabited and expanded. The critics of the b-school who inhabit the b-school are one obvious example. Though they might be ticks on an elephant, and the elephant barely notices, they show us that organization is never totalizing, never complete and finished. So it will be with the school for organizing, which will be criticized from within and without, as it should be.

ORGANIZING NEVER ENDS: INCONCLUSION

It might be that forms of organizing are as wildly different as our imaginations will allow, as my small example of a German cola manufacturer illustrates. The Brazilian political and legal theorist and politician Roberto Mangabeira Unger captures this nicely as an 'experimental' attitude to social organization.[16] If we assume, he says, that social life is always built from certain 'formative contexts', then radical social innovation within any era becomes possible only if these contexts can be 'denaturalized', or 'disentrenched'. That is to say, Unger wants to acknowledge that all knowledge and practice is socially located, at the same time that he insists that it is not socially determined, and that there is no necessary logic to history. He thinks that the biggest danger is what he calls 'false necessity', the idea that the world must take a certain shape because of some suggested laws of human action or development. This is an argument against any particular teleology, and for the collective development of (borrowing the term from John Keats) a sense of 'negative capability', the capacity to think in a way that contradicts the formative contexts that we find ourselves in, that imaginatively posits new ways of thinking about ourselves and our social relations. Thinking outside the box, if that cliché may be allowed, and if the box is the b-school.

The reason I find Unger's ideas relevant (and inspiring) here is largely because he insists that everything is political. That is to say, that forms of social organization should never be treated as somehow outside or beyond politics – driven by mere efficiency or functional necessity – but instead as examples of what I have called 'organizing as politics made durable'. This term is meant to gesture towards the ways in which any form of organizing represents the solidification of assumptions about the capacities of different sorts of human beings, and the relations that they should have with each other. Unger often uses the example of

the work organization in order to explore questions of legitimacy
and authority, and to question the necessity of what he calls the
'English path' to a particular form of hierarchically managed
stockholder company. More generally, he is trying to think against
what he calls 'frozen politics', the congealing of possibility into
necessity, even inevitability. Because once social arrangements
are frozen, whether in the shape of a corporation or any other
form, they become a sort of solidified common sense, a tableau
of static relations. This seems to me to fit well with Chantal
Mouffe's agonistic assumptions about 'the political' as a ground
of contestation upon which the grubby business of politics takes
place.[17] For both Unger and Mouffe, politics doesn't end in a
particular institution, in nouns, but is a verb to which we must
continually be attentive.

The same, I think, is true of organization. This book would
be digging its own grave if I concluded by suggesting that the
foundation of a new university department will solve all the
problems that we face. This is not just a question of reforming
the business school, as if this were the only game in town, but
rather a wider issue of encouraging organizational experiments
and the contexts that make them possible. The legal and institutional frameworks which cradle different organizational
forms are vitally important here, particularly those which enable
arrangements which are collective in their financing, governance
and sharing of gains.[18] The school for organizing will necessarily
concentrate on organizations, but sustained consideration of
the policy environment which produces an ecology which is
hospitable to experiments will be essential too. More generally
though, I believe that we need to begin with a strong assumption
about organizational variety, an encyclopaedia of alternatives,
and then evaluate different sorts of institutions in a way that is
informed by normative discussions. In this, questions of means
and ends becomes important. A company that manufactures
highly caffeinated cola, but does so with remarkably democratic

forms of governance, might be compared to a company that produces locally sourced lentil-based snacks, but demonstrates autocratic forms of management and uses precarious labour. As we saw in Chapter 8, practices and intentions, means and ends, will need to be evaluated separately and together, and on a variety of criteria – for example, whether they produce community, whether they allow autonomy, and whether they demonstrate responsibility to other humans and non-humans. The butterfly collecting of variety and multiplicity is not a good in itself, but it is the necessary ground for discussions about the normative commitments and consequences of different forms of organizing, in just the same way that Chantal Mouffe's ontology of 'the political' is the ground for discussions about political strategy and tactics. After all, we need to see the alternatives in order to realize that there are choices.

Universities can't change the world, so we shouldn't overstate the importance of a new form of business school, even one with a new name and tasty new filling. There are wider structural determinations at work here, forces which will resist as well as incorporate. If it gets noticed at all, this book will be the subject of ridicule, perhaps dismissed as no more than a plea for more business ethics and CSR modules. Its failure is already assured. But to demand success as the end of political intervention and invention is to mistake an end for a means. This is why I find Unger's call for a radical extension of politics to be so helpful, because it begins to push back the false necessities that tell us that the world just has to be some particular way. The forms of corporate managerialism which subordinate ethics and politics to assertions about the bottom line are politics too after all, most particularly in their attempt to insist that politics doesn't belong in the boardroom, on the factory floor, in the supply chain, or the supermarket. Organizational arrangements are always politics congealed into rules and routines, the entrenchment of assumptions about who decides and who benefits. In order to compare them, it is necessary to begin by assuming difference and variety rather than uniformity, and continuously interrogating all organizational arrangements for their open and hidden politics. The endless turbulence of an ontology of the political cannot be evaded with false necessities, with a brittle and frozen politics produced by antipolitics machines, so let's celebrate and explore multiplicity, and imagine the fantastic worlds we might create together. Let's bulldoze the business school.

Notes

PREFACE

1. For those who are interested, I think that this book is probably the last one in a set of four. It began with *Against Management* (Cambridge: Polity, 2002), particularly the last chapter in that volume, titled 'For organization'. The exploration of alternatives continued in *The Dictionary of Alternatives* (edited with Valerie Fournier and Patrick Reedy, London: Zed 2007), and the *Companion to Alternatives* (edited with George Cheney, Valerie Fournier and Chris Land, London: Routledge 2014). This book completes that set, I hope. I really don't want to do another one.

CHAPTER I

1. Wright, L. (1939) 'Some Early "Friends" of Libraries' *Huntingdon Library Quarterly* 2/3: 355–369.
2. www.wbs.ac.uk/about/difference/mission/, accessed 15 September 2014.
3. Douglas, M. (1987) *How Institutions Think*. London: Routledge and Kegan Paul.
4. Just as deliciously, in 2000, Imperial College, University of London, accepted £27 million from the US businessman Gary Tanaka, in return for naming rights for their business school. In 2008 he was found guilty of securities fraud and sentenced to five years in jail. Coincidentally, the business school changed its name in 2008.
5. This is pre-dated by the Aula do Comércio in Lisbon which opened in 1759 and closed in 1844, but it appears to have only taught accounting.
6. Touzet, L. and Corbeil, P. (2015) 'Vital Roux, Forgotten Forerunner of Modern Business Games' *Simulation & Gaming* 46/1: 19–39.
7. Ibid.
8. Augier, M. and March, J.G. (2011) *The Roots, Rituals and Rhetorics of Change: North American Business Schools after the Second World War*. Stanford, CA, Stanford Business Books, p. 158.
9. Thomas, H., Lorange, P., and Sheth, J. (2013) *The Business School in the 21st Century*. Cambridge: Cambridge University Press, p. 5.

10. Pettigrew, A. and Starkey, K. (2016) 'The Legitimacy and Impact of Business Schools' *Academy of Management Learning and Education* 15/4: 649–664, 652.

11. Thomas et al. (2013) *The Business School in the 21st Century*, p. 107.

12. Ibid., 268.

13. See, respectively, Steyaert, C., Beyes, T., and Parker, M. (eds) (2016) *The Companion to Reinventing Management Education.* London: Routledge; Khurana, R. (2007) *From Higher Aims to Hired Hands. The Social Transformation of American Business Schools and the Unfulfilled Promise of Management as a Profession.* Princeton, NJ: Princeton University Press; O'Connor, E. (2012) *Creating New Knowledge in Management, Appropriating the Field's Lost Foundations.* Stanford, CA: Stanford University Press; Augier and March, *Roots, Rituals and Rhetorics.*

14. Harney, S. (2007) 'Socialization and the b-school' *Management Learning* 38/2: 139–153.

15. See, for some examples of what is now a mountain of paper, Alvesson, M., and Willmott, H. (eds) (1992), *Critical Management Studies.* London: Sage; Alvesson, M., Bridgman, T. and Willmott, H. (eds) (2009) *The Oxford Handbook of Critical Management Studies.* Oxford: Oxford University Press; Alvesson, M. (ed.) (2011) *Classics in Critical Management Studies.* Cheltenham: Edward Elgar; Klikauer, T. (2013) *Managerialism: A Critique of an Ideology.* London: Palgrave Macmillan; Prasad, A., Prasad, P., Mills, A. and Helms Mills, J. (eds) (2016), *The Routledge Companion to Critical Management Studies,* London and New York: Routledge. On applying some of these ideas to the business school, see Campbell Jones and Damian O'Doherty (eds) (2005) *Manifestos for the Business School of Tomorrow.* Finland: Dvalin; Tony Huzzard, Mats Benner and Dan Kärreman (eds) (2017) *The Corporatization of the Business School.* London: Routledge.

16. Parker, M. (2001) 'Fucking Management: Queer, Theory and Reflexivity' *ephemera* 1/1: 36-53; Parker, M. (2002) *Against Management.* Oxford: Polity; Holbrook, M. (2013) 'The greedy bastards guide to business' *Journal of Macromarketing* 33/4: 369–385. The quote is from the introduction to Jones and O'Doherty (2005) *Manifestos,* p. 1.

CHAPTER 2

1. Snyder, Benson R. (1971) *The Hidden Curriculum.* New York: Alfred A. Knopf.

2. Parker, M. (2015) 'Between sociology and the b school: Critical studies of organization, work and employment in the UK' *Sociological Review* 63/1: 162–180.

3. A good example of what organizational theorists call 'institutional isomorphism'. See McKiernan, P. and Wilson, D. (2014) 'Strategic choice: Taking "business" out of b-schools'. In Pettigrew, A. et al. (eds) *The Institutional Development of Business Schools*. Oxford: Oxford University Press.

4. A fact asserted in a remarkably dreadful book allegedly assessing b-school education: Thomas, H., Lorange, P., and Sheth, J. (2013) *The Business School in the Twenty-First Century*. Cambridge: Cambridge University Press.

CHAPTER 3

1. Jacques, R. (1996) *Manufacturing the Employee: Management Knowledge from the 19th to the 21st Centuries*. London: Sage.

2. Of course other starting points could have been chosen: the arsenale at Venice, the Jesuits, a slave plantation, the construction of a canal, the Springfield Armoury, West Point Military Academy or a railway company. History rarely has clear places where things begin.

3. Weber, M. (1948) *For Max Weber*, eds H.H. Gerth and C. Wright Mills. London: Routledge and Kegan Paul. The quotes are on pp. 214, 215–216 and 218 respectively.

4. The references are Arendt, H. (1963/1994) *Eichmann in Jerusalem: A Report on the Banality of Evil*. London: Penguin; Whyte, W.H. (1961) *The Organization Man*. Harmondsworth: Penguin; Marcuse, H. (1964) *One Dimensional Man*. London: Routledge and Kegan Paul; Vaneigem, R. (1992) *The Revolution of Everyday Life*. London: Left Bank Books & Rebel Press; MacIntyre, A. (1981) *After Virtue*. London: Duckworth; Bauman, Z. (1989) *Modernity and the Holocaust*. Oxford: Polity; Debord, G. (1967/1995) *The Society of the Spectacle*. New York: Zone Books. Quote is from Vaneigem (1992) *The Revolution of Everyday Life*, pp. 52, 55.

5. Protherough, R. and Pick, J. (2002) *Managing Britannia. Culture and Management in Modern Britain*. Norfolk: Edgeways, Brynmill Press; Ritzer, G. (2000) *The McDonaldization of Society*. London: Sage.

6. For a left intellectual example of a similar argument, see Wheen, F. (2004) *How Mumbo Jumbo Conquered the World*. London. Fourth Estate.

7. Protherough and Pick (2002) *Managing Britannia*, p. 42.

8. Shirky, C. (2008) *Here Comes Everybody. The Power of Organizing Without Organizations*. London: Penguin; Frank, T. (1998) *The Conquest of Cool: Business Culture, Counterculture, and the Rise of Hip*

Consumerism. Chicago, IL: University of Chicago Press; Frank, T. (2000) *One Market Under God*. London: Secker and Warburg.

9. In Starkey, K. and Tiratsoo, N. (2007) *The Business School and the Bottom Line*. Cambridge: Cambridge University Press.

10. See Parker, M. (2005) 'Organisational Gothic' *Culture and Organization* 11/3: 153–166; (2006) 'The counter culture of organisation: Towards a cultural studies of representations of work' *Consumption, Markets and Culture* 9/1: 1–15; *Alternative Business: Outlaws, Crime and Culture*. London: Routledge.

11. Bierce, A. (1911) *The Devil's Dictionary*. /www.thedevilsdictionary.com/?c=#!

12. Josephson, on p. 53 of Beder, S. (2000) *Selling the Work Ethic: From Puritan Pulpit to Corporate PR*. London: Zed Books.

13. Compare this with the seventeenth-century idea of the 'projector'. See Hamilton, V. and Parker, M. (2016) *Daniel Defoe and the Bank of England*. Alresford, Hants: ZerO Books.

14. Marshall, P. (1993) *Demanding the Impossible: A History of Anarchism*. London: Fontana; Parker, M., Cheney, G., Fournier, V. and Land, C. (2014) 'The question of organization: A manifesto for alternatives', *ephemera* [www.ephemeraweb.org] 14/4: 623–638.

15. The inclusion of the word 'management' in this phrase tells us something about some of its assumptions about scale and hierarchy. See Vanek, J. (ed.) (1975) *Self-Management: Economic Liberation of Man*. Harmondsworth: Penguin; Albert, M. and Hahnel, R. (1991) *Looking Forward: Participatory Economics for the 21st Century*. Cambridge, MA: South End Press; Rocker, R. (2004) *Anarcho-Syndicalism: Theory and Practice*. Oakland, CA: AK Press.

16. Cahn, E. (2000) *No More Throw Away People: The Co-production Imperative*. Washington, DC: Essential Books; Erdal, D. (2011) *Beyond the Corporation: Humanity Working*. London: The Bodley Head; Atzeni, M. (ed.) (2012) *Alternative Work Organizations*. London: Palgrave Macmillan; Novkovic, S. and Webb, T. (eds) (2014) *Co-operatives in a Post Growth Era*. London: Zed Books.

17. On Goldman, see Marshall, *Demanding the Impossible*, p. 396. More generally see Ferree, M. and Martin, P. (1995) *Feminist Organizations*. Philadelphia, PA: Temple University Press. On bureaucracy see Bologh, R. (1990) *Love or Greatness: Max Weber and Masculine Thinking*. London: Unwin Hyman.

18. Naess, A. (1989) *Ecology, Community and Lifestyle*. Cambridge: Cambridge University Press; Warren, K. (ed.) (1997) *Ecofeminism*.

Bloomington: Indiana University Press; Bookchin, M. (1997) *The Murray Bookchin Reader*. New York: Continuum International Publishing.

CHAPTER 4

1. Starkey, K. and Tiratsoo, N. (2007) *The Business School and the Bottom Line*. Cambridge: Cambridge University Press, 7; Alajoutsijärvi, K., Juusola, K. and Siltaoja, M. (2015) 'The legitimacy paradox of business schools: Losing by gaining', *Academy of Management Learning and Education* 14/2: 277–291. See pp. 64 *passim* in Thomas, H., Lorange, P. and Sheth, J. (2013) *The Business School in the Twenty-First Century*. Cambridge: Cambridge University Press, for a typical summary of these complaints.
2. Caulkin, S. (2008) 'When it came to the crunch, MBAs didn't help' *Guardian* 26 October; Podolny, J. (2009) 'The buck stops (and starts) at Business School' *Harvard Business Review*, June: 62–67; Walker, P. (2009) 'Who taught them greed is good?' *Guardian* 8 March; *The Economist* (2009) 'The pedagogy of the privileged', 24 September. See also Tett, G. (2009) *Fool's Gold*. London: Abacus.
3. Locke, R. (1996) *The Collapse of the American Management Mystique*. Oxford: Oxford University Press; Parker, M. (2002) *Against Management*. Oxford: Polity; Bennis, W. and O'Toole, J. (2005) 'How business schools lost their way', *Harvard Business Review* 83/5: 96–104; Ghoshal, S. (2005) 'Bad management theories are destroying good management practices' *Academy of Management Learning and Education* 4/1: 75–91.
4. For an early example of someone who didn't share the notion of a golden age of the technocratic business school, see C. Wright Mills's 1948 essay, 'The contribution of sociology to studies of industrial relations'. It was republished in 1970 in the *Berkeley Journal of Sociology* 15: 11–32.
5. Khurana, R. (2007) *From Higher Aims to Hired Hands. The Social Transformation of American Business Schools and the Unfulfilled Promise of Management as a Profession*. Princeton, NJ: Princeton University Press; Augier, M. and March, J.G. (2011) *The Roots, Rituals and Rhetorics of Change: North American Business Schools after the Second World War*. Stanford, CA: Stanford Business Books; O'Connor, E. (2012) *Creating New Knowledge in Management, Appropriating the Field's Lost Foundations*. Stanford, CA: Stanford University Press.

6. Ghoshal (2005) 'Bad management theories': 76. See also Locke, R. and Spender, J.-C. (2011) *Confronting Managerialism: How the Business Elite and their Schools Threw Our Life Out of Balance.* London: Zed Books.

7. Colby, A., Ehrlich, T., Sullivan, W. and Dolle, J. (2011) *Rethinking Undergraduate Business Education.* San Francisco, CA: Jossey-Bass. For various responses, see Steyaert, C., Beyes, T., and Parker, M. (eds) (2016) *The Companion to Reinventing Management Education,* and for a radical account, see Harney, S. and Thomas, H. (2013) 'Towards a liberal management education' *Journal of Management Development* 32/5: 508–524.

8. Mintzberg, H. (2004) *Managers not MBAs.* London: Pearson Education.

9. Khurana, R. and Nohria, N. (2008) 'It's time to make management a true profession' *Harvard Business Review,* October: 70–77.

10. Podolny (2009) 'The buck stops (and starts) at Business School': 65–66.

11. Anteby, M. (2013) *Manufacturing Morals: The Values of Silence in Business Education.* Chicago, IL: University of Chicago Press. On Harvard more generally, see McDonald, D. (2017) *The Golden Passport* New York: HarperCollins.

12. See pp. 105 *passim* in Starkey and Tiratsoo (2007) *The Business School and the Bottom Line;* Losada, C., Martell, J. and Lozano, J. (2011) 'Responsible business education' in Morsing, M. and Sauquet Rovira, A. (eds) (2011) *Business Schools and their Contribution to Society.* London: Sage, for reviews of these studies. On the instrumentalism of students, see Rynes, S., Lawson, M. and Ilies, R. (2003) 'Behavioural coursework in business education' *Academy of Management Learning and Education* 2/3: 442–56.

13. *Economist* (2009) 'The pedagogy of the privileged'. See also Crossean, M. et al. (2013) 'Developing leadership character in business programs' *Academy of Management Learning and Education* 12: 285–305.

14. In its latest version, the 'debate' begins with Pfeffer, J. and Fong, C. (2002) 'The end of business schools: Less success than meets the eye' *Academy of Management Learning and Education* 1/1: 78–95; and is amply summarized in Keiser, A., Nicolai, A. and Seidl, D. (2015) 'The practical relevance of management research' *Academy of Management Annals* 9/1: 143–233.

15. Allen, A. (2017) *The Cynical Educator.* Leicester: Mayfly Books, p. 8.

16. See, for a nicely expressed selection of these complaints, with chapters on audit, accreditation, writing, branding, editing, employability and

so on, Huzzard, T., Benner, M. and Kärreman, D. (eds) (2017) *The Corporatization of the Business School*. London: Routledge.

17. Akrivou, K. and Bradbury-Huang, H. (2015) 'Educating integrated catalysts: Transforming business schools towards ethics and sustainability' *Academy of Management Learning and Education* 14/2: 222–240.

CHAPTER 5

1. Augier, M. and March, J.G. (2011) *The Roots, Rituals and Rhetorics of Change: North American Business Schools after the Second World War*. Stanford, CA, Stanford Business Books, p. 4.
2. For an excellent review of the modern global university, see Collini, S. (2012) *What are Universities For?* London: Penguin.
3. Pettigrew, A. and Starkey, K. (2016) 'From the guest editors: The legitimacy and impact of business schools – key issues and a research agenda' *Academy of Management Learning and Education* 15/4: 649–664.
4. When I was a head of department of a small management school in a UK university, I was required to go to training about leadership delivered by outside consultants. The content was at about the same level that I would deliver on a first-year lecture, so I said so. I was then accused of being disruptive by a deputy vice chancellor. The fact that I taught about management did not make me an expert in its local practice.
5. Parker, M. and Jary, D. (1995) 'The McUniversity: Organization, management and academic subjectivity' *Organization* 2/2: 319–338.
6. Subramaniam, M., Perrucci, R. and Whitlock, D. (2014) 'Intellectual closure: A theoretical framework linking knowledge, power and the corporate university' *Critical Sociology* 40/3: 411–430.
7. Readings, B. (1996) *The University in Ruins*. Cambridge, MA: Harvard University Press; Johnson, B., Kavanagh, P. and Mattson, K. (eds) (2003) *Steal This University: The Rise of the Corporate University and the Academic Labor Movement*. New York: Routledge; Slaughter, S. and Rhoades, G. (2004) *Academic Capitalism and the New Economy*. Baltimore, MD: John Hopkins University Press.

CHAPTER 6

1. For reasons that I can't fathom, in the UK the title 'Management School' is often believed to refer to something more academic – more university and less trade – than the 'Business School'. When a

management school turns into a business school, it often causes a lot of fuss amongst those academics who believe that they shouldn't be captured by business.

2. See Jackson, N. and Carter, P. (1998) 'Labour as dressage'. In McKinlay, A. and Starkey, K. (eds) *Foucault, Management and Organization Theory*. London: Sage, pp. 49–64.

3. *The London Encyclopaedia or Universal Dictionary* (1829) Volume 13. London: Thomas Tegg, p. 498.

4. http://www.bbc.co.uk/news/magazine-23462290, accessed 5 November 2017.

5. An endnote for my friends. I know this is an exaggeration, but how much of what we have done over the past 25 years has explored alternatives, either within education or practice?

6. Read, H. (1963/2002) 'The cult of leadership'. In idem, *To Hell with Culture, and Other Essays on Art and Society*. London: Routledge, pp. 48–69.

7. A reference to the *Thomas the Tank Engine* stories, for those who have never had the pleasure.

CHAPTER 7

1. Hardt, M. and Negri, T. (2009) *Commonwealth*, Cambridge, MA: Belknap Press, p. 238.

2. Kalika, M., Shenton, G. and Dubois, P. (2016) 'What happens if a business school disappears?' *Journal of Management Development* 35/7: 878–888.

3. McKiernan, P. and Wilson, D. (2014) 'Strategic choice: Taking "business" out of b-schools'. In Pettigrew, A. et al. (eds) *The Institutional Development of Business Schools*. Oxford: Oxford University Press.

4. In late 2016, a UK School of Organizing was beginning, though it has no website. It's called the Ella Baker School of Organizing and is dedicated to studying historical forms of community and trade union organization.

5. For some more sophisticated accounts of this process, and its reverse, see Burrell, G. and Parker, M. (eds) (2016) *For Robert Cooper: Collected Work*. London: Routledge.

6. Co-operatives UK (2017) 'Reimagine the economy. The UK co-operative economy 2017'. http://reports.uk.coop/economy2017/

7. In Roper, J. (2016) 'Case study: Total pay equality and multi-skilling at a workers' co-operative', *HR Magazine* 1 September, www.hrmagazine. co.uk/article-details/case-study-total-equality-of-pay-and-multi-

skilling-at-a-workers-co-operative. Also see Suma's website, www. suma.coop/ and Jones, D. (2000) 'Leadership strategies for sustainable development: A case study of Suma Wholefood' *Business Strategy and the Environment* 9/6: 378–389; Ridley-Duff, R.J. (2009) 'Cooperative social enterprises: Company rules, access to finance and management practice', *Social Enterprise Journal*, 5/1: 50–68; Cannell, B. (2015) 'Doing it the hard way?' *Co-ops UK Blog*, https://www.uk.coop/ newsroom/bob-cannell-doing-it-hard-way.

8. See, for some accounts of these differences, the first section in Morsing, M. and Sauquet Rovira, A. (2011) *Business Schools and Their Contribution to Society*. London: Sage. Also Alves, M. and Pozzebon, M. (2013) 'How to resist linguistic domination and promote knowledge diversity?' *Revists de Administração de Empresas* 53/6: 629–633, and McKiernan and Wilson (2014) 'Strategic choice', pp. 264 *passim*.

9. Ghoshal, S. (2005) 'Bad management theories are destroying good management practices' *Academy of Management Learning and Education* 4/1: 75–91.

10. Starkey, K. and Hatchuel, A. (2014) 'Back to the future of management research'. In Pettigrew, A. et al. (eds) *The Institutional Development of Business Schools*. Oxford: Oxford University Press.

11. Starkey, K. and Tiratsoo, N. (2007) *The Business School and the Bottom Line*. Cambridge: Cambridge University Press, 212.

12. Parker, M., Fournier, V. and Reedy, P. (2007) *The Dictionary of Alternatives: Utopianism and Organization*. London: Zed Books.

13. And yes, I still have them, in case some publisher wants them one day.

CHAPTER 8

1. Attributed to the labour organizer Joe Hill. http://en.wikipedia.org/ wiki/Joe_Hill

2. Thanks to Valerie Fournier, George Cheney and Chris Land for their collaboration on earlier versions of the arguments in this chapter.

3. Michels, R. (1915) *Political Parties: A Sociological Study of the Oligarchical Tendencies of Modern Democracy.* New York: The Free Press.

4. Lovink, G. and Scholz, T. (2007) *The Art of Free Cooperation*. Brooklyn, NY: Autonomedia; Maeckelbergh, M. (2011) 'Doing is believing: Prefiguration as strategic practice in the alterglobalization movement'. *Social Movement Studies*, 10/1: 1–20.

5. Mill, J.S. (1859/2005) *On Liberty*. New York: Cosimo Classics; Nozick, R. (1974) *Anarchy, State and Utopia*. New York: Basic Books.

6. Macintyre, A. (1981) *After Virtue*. London: Duckworth; Marx, K. and Engels, F. (1967) *The Communist Manifesto*. Harmondsworth: Penguin; Mulhall, S. and Swift, A. (1992) *Liberals and Communitarians*. Oxford: Blackwell.

7. Berlin, I. (1969) *Two Concepts of Liberty*. Oxford: Clarendon Press.

8. Bauman, Z. (1989) *Modernity and the Holocaust*. Cambridge: Polity; Bauman, Z. (2007) *Liquid Times*. Cambridge: Polity.

9. Bakunin, M. (1867) 'Federalism, socialism, anti-theologism' https://www.marxists.org/reference/archive/bakunin/works/various/reasons-of-state.htm

10. Burke, Edmund (1790) *Reflections on The Revolution in France.*

11. Constitution of the Iroquois Nations http://www.indigenouspeople.net/iroqcon.htm

12. To rephrase Bruno Latour (1991) 'Technology is society made durable'. In J. Law (ed.) *A Sociology of Monsters? Essays on Power, Technology and Domination*. London: Routledge, pp. 103–131.

13. Gibson-Graham, J.K. (1996) *The End of Capitalism (As We Knew It)*. Cambridge: Blackwell; Gibson-Graham, J.K. (2006) *A Postcapitalist Politics*. Minneapolis: University of Minnesota Press; Gibson-Graham, J.K. (2013) *Take Back the Economy*. Minneapolis: University of Minnesota Press; Williams, C. (2005) *A Commodified World? Mapping the Limits of Capitalism*. London: Zed Books.

14. Mouffe, C. (2013) *Agonistics: Thinking the World Politically*, Verso, London. See, for an application, Parker, S. and Parker, M. (2017) 'Antagonism, accommodation and agonism in Critical Management Studies: Alternative organizations as allies' *Human Relations* 53(1): 7–32.

15. Scott, J.C. (2012) *Two Cheers for Anarchism.* Princeton, NJ: Princeton University Press, p. 111.

CHAPTER 9

1. On rankings and branding in business schools, see the chapters by Enders and by Rasche et al. in Pettigrew, A., Cornuel, E. and Hommel, U. (eds) (2014) *The Institutional Development of Business Schools*. Oxford: Oxford University Press.

2. There are plenty of problems with this statement, particularly for anyone who knows about the radical philosophies of Paulo Friere, Ivan Illich, or Jacques Rancière. In my defence, none of them would be keen on market-based solutions which made students into customers either.

3. Though there are actually very few goods that are completely private. The consumption of too many cheeseburgers has effects which can become a public health issue. The purchasing of cheap clothing from non-unionized suppliers in the Global South helps maintain a market for 'sweatshop' production. And so on.

4. www.unprme.org/about-prme/the-six-principles.php

5. And that will probably be Ca' Foscari in Venice, unless anyone can tell me differently.

6. Jameson, F. (2003) 'Future city', *New Left Review*, 21(May/June): 65–79.

7. Something that Jameson also speculates on in *Archaeologies of the Future: The Desire Called Utopia and Other Science Fictions* (London: Verso, 2007), in which he suggests that fantastic imaginings are a sublimated desire for social change. See also my *Alternative Business: Outlaws, Crime and Culture* (Routledge 2012) on why Robin Hood and Captain Jack Sparrow can also be understood as examples of the critique in culture.

8. Benson, P. and Kirsch, S. (2010) 'Capitalism and the politics of resignation' *Current Anthropology* 51/4: 459–486, at p. 475.

9. https://quoteinvestigator.com/2017/03/28/future/

CHAPTER 10

1. This lovely title is stolen from a paper which foreshadowed the technocratic era of the business school in the US by insisting that management specialists should be teaching about quantitative techniques of management: Bach, G.L. (1958) 'Some observations on the business school of tomorrow', *Management Science* 4/4: 351–364.

2. Eagleton, T. (2000) 'Utopia and its opposites', in Panitch, L. and Leys, C. (eds) *Socialist Register* 36, p. 31.

3. Brickell, C. (ed.) (1993) *The Royal Horticultural Society Gardener's Encyclopedia of Plants and Flowers*. London: Dorling Kindersley, p. 5.

4. Bauman, Z. (1989) *Modernity and the Holocaust*. Cambridge: Polity; Scott, J. (1998) *Seeing Like a State*. New Haven, CT: Yale University Press.

5. For some other versions of what the business school of the future might look like, see Ferlie, E., McGivern, G. and De Moraes, A. (2010) 'Developing a public interest school of management', *British Journal of Management* 21/1: 60–70; https://www.cardiff.ac.uk/__data/assets/pdf_file/0008/572732/The-Public-Value-Business-School.pdf for the 'public value' business school; or for a social science version of this idea,

Delbridge, R. (2014) 'Promising futures: CMS, post-disciplinarity, and the new public social science', *Journal of Management Studies* 51/1: 95–117. For some wilder and less systematic speculations, have a look at Jones, C. and O'Doherty, D. (eds) (2005) *Manifestos for the Business School of Tomorrow*. Finland: Dvalin.

6. Or at least, pretty much like a sociology department. Several commentators have suggested that is really my aim here, a colonization of the b-school by sociology.

7. I am aware that I have said very little in this book about how business schools teach, being primarily concerned with what they teach. For some ideas on the former, see Mingers, J. (2000) 'What is it to be critical?' *Management Learning* 31/2: 219–237, as well as many of the chapters in Steyaert, C., Beyes, T. and Parker, M. (eds) (2016) *The Companion to Reinventing Management Education*. London: Routledge. An application of alternatives to the curriculum can be found in Reedy, P. and Learmonth, M. (2009) 'Other possibilities? The contribution to management education of alternative organizations' *Management Learning* 40/3: 241–258.

8. Starkey, K. and Hatchuel, A. (2014) 'Back to the future of management research'. In Pettigrew, A. et al. (eds) *The Institutional Development of Business Schools*. Oxford: Oxford University Press.

9. Ibid., p. 290. For a nice essay on the necessary tensions between inside and outside, discipline and profession, see Irwin, A. (2017) 'Mixing oil and water', in Huzzard, T., Benner, M. and Kärreman, D. (eds) (2017) *The Corporatization of the Business School*. London: Routledge, pp. 217–233.

10. A phrase I have stolen and adapted from Irwin, A., Salskov-Iversen, D. and Morsing, M. (2011) 'Business schools in society', in Morsing, M. and Sauquet Rovira, A. (2011) *Business Schools and Their Contribution to Society*. London: Sage, p. 75.

11. www.premium-cola.de/. For research on the organization, see www.premium-cola.de/betriebssystem/wissenschaft and http://wiki.premium-cola.de/betriebssystem/untersuchungen. Thanks to Uwe Lubberman for conversations about the collective.

12. See, for example, Shirky, C. (2008) *Here Comes Everybody. The Power of Organizing Without Organizations*. London: Penguin; and Nunes, R. (2014) *Organizations of the Organizationless. Collective Action After Networks*. Lüneberg, Germany: Leuphana University: Post-Media Lab/Mute.

13. Illich, I. (1971) *Deschooling Society*. New York: Harper and Row.

14. Nunes (2014) *Organizations of the Organizationless*.

15. Harney, S. and Moten, F. (2013) *The Undercommons: Fugitive Planning and Black Study*. Wivenhoe: Minor Compositions.

16. Unger, R. (1998) *Democracy Realized: The Progressive Alternative*. London: Verso and *idem* (2004) *False Necessity: Anti-Neccessitarian Social Theory in the Service of Radical Democracy*. London: Verso. See, for an argument with a similar ambition, Wright, E.O. (2010) *Envisioning Real Utopias*. London: Verso.

17. Mouffe, C. (2013) *Agonistics: Thinking the World Politically*. London: Verso.

18. For a very sketchy discussion of what an economy that encouraged small-scale alternatives might look like, see Parker, M. (2017) 'Alternative enterprises, local economies, and social justice: Why smaller is still more beautiful' *M@n@gement*. 20/4: 418–434.

Index